I0132012

D. Sime

The Edinburgh Musical Miscellany

A Collection of the most Approved Scotch, English, and Irish songs, set to music -

Vol. 1

D. Sime

The Edinburgh Musical Miscellany
A Collection of the most Approved Scotch, English, and Irish songs, set to music - Vol. 1

ISBN/EAN: 9783337126483

Printed in Europe, USA, Canada, Australia, Japan

Cover: Foto ©Thomas Meinert / pixelio.de

More available books at **www.hansebooks.com**

THE

EDINBURGH

MUSICAL MISCELLANY:

A

COLLECTION

OF THE MOST APPROVED

SCOTCH, ENGLISH, AND IRISH

SONGS,

SET TO MUSIC.

SELECTED BY *D. SIME,* EDINBURGH.

EDINBURGH:

Printed for W. Gordon, T. Brown, N. R. Cheyne,
C. Elliot, & Silvester Doig, *Edinburgh;* W. Coke,
Leith; J. Gillies, *Glasgow;* & G. Milln,
& W. Brown, *Dundee.*

MDCCXCII.

PREFACE.

THE Editor of this Volume pre-
fents it to the Public as containing a felection of the moft approved Songs, on different fubjects, fu-
perior, it is hoped, to any thing
of the kind that has hitherto appeared in this Country. In com-
piling it, particular attention has
been paid, more, perhaps, than
in any other publication of the
fame kind, to the fetts of the
different airs, and the correctnefs
of the mufic, which ought to be

the principal recommendation in a work of this nature.

FROM the variety of the fubjects felected, he flatters himfelf, alfo, that every lover of Harmony will find a certain number adapted to his particular tafte. A place has been impartially given to the Scots, Englifh, and Irifh Songs, which have been confidered, by the ableft judges, as poffeffing the greateft merit : and, from this circumftance, one great advantage will arife,----the giving an opportunity of comparing the particular character and genius of the different countries.

In

IN this Collection will be found, what has never appeared in any former Mifcellany, many of the celebrated and much admired fongs of Arne, Dibdin, Shield, Arnold, Hook, &c. by which the Public are put in poffeffion of a number of the neweft pieces, that before this could only be had feparately, at a high purchafe : And, from the profeffional abilities of the Compiler, it may be further added, that this Volume can be prefented with a confidence fuch publications hitherto have not been entitled to.

The

CONTENTS.

D

CONTENTS. ix

Y

MUSICAL MISCELLANY.

SONG I.

TO ANACREON IN HEAVEN.

SUNG BY MR BANNISTER AT THE ANACREONTIC SOCIETY.

To Anacreon in heaven, where he fat in full glee,

A few fons of harmony fent a petition, That he

their infpirer and patron would be : When this

anfwer arriv'd from the jol-ly old Grecian :—

Voice, fiddle, and flute, no longer be mute, I'll

lend you my name, and infpire you to boot ; and

befides I'll inftruct you like me to entwine the

myrtle of Venus with Bacchus's vine. *And be-*

fides I'll inftruct you like me to entwine the myrtle of

Venus with Bacchus's vine.

The news through Olympus immediately flew :
When Old Thunder pretended to give himfelf airs,—
" If thefe mortals are fuffer'd their fcheme to purfue,
" The devil a Goddefs will ftay above ftairs.
    " Hark ! already they cry,
    " In tranfports of joy,
  " Away to the fons of Anacreon we'll fly,
" And there with good fellows we'll learn to entwine
" The myrtle of Venus with Bacchus's vine.
    And there with good fellows, &c.

" The yellow-hair'd God, and his nine fufty maids,
" From Helicon's Banks will incontinent flee,
" Idalia will boaft but of tenantlefs fhades,
  " And the bi-forked hill a mere defert will be.
    " My thunder, no fear on't,
    " Shall foon do its errand,   [warrant,
" And dam'me! I'll fwinge the ringleaders, I
" I'll trim the young dogs for thus daring to twine
" The myrtle of Venus with Bacchus's vine."
    I'll trim the young dogs, &c.

Apollo rofe up, and faid, " Pr'ythee ne'er quarrel,
  " Good King of the Gods, with my vot'ries below:
" Your thunder is ufclefs"---then fhewing his laurel,
Cry'd " *Sic evitabile fulmen,* you know!
    " Then over each head,
    " My laurels I'll fpread;   [dread,
" So my fons from your crackers no mifchief fhall
" Whilft fnug in their club-room they jovially twine
" The myrtle of Venus with Bacchus's vine.
    Whilft fnug in their club-room, &c.

Next Momus got up with his rifible phiz,
  And fwore with Apollo he'd cheerfully join---
" The tide of full harmony ftill fhall be his,   [mine.
  " But the fong, and the catch, and the laugh fhall be,
    " Then Jove, be not jealous
    " Of thefe honeft fellows."
Cry'd Jove, " We relent, fince the truth you now
    " tell us;

" And fwear, by Old Styx, that they long fhal'
" entwine
" The myrtle of Venus with Bacchus's vine."

And fwear, by old Styx, &c.

Ye fons of Anacreon, then, join hand in hand :
Preferve unanimity, friendfhip, and love ;
'Tis your's to fupport what's fo happily plann'd :
You're the fanction of Gods, and the fiat of Jove.
      While thus we agree,
      Our toaft let it be,
May our club flourifh happy, united, and free !
And long may the fons of Anacreon entwine
The myrtle of Venus with Bacchus's vine.

And long may the fons of Anacreon entwine
The myrtle of Venus with Bacchus's vine.

SONG II.

FOR A LITERARY SOCIETY, CALLED

" THE SOCIAL CLUB."

TUNE---" TO ANACREON IN HEAVEN."

Omne tulit Punctum, qui mifcuit utile dulci.   HOR.

ON azure-wove couches as the Gods lay reclin'd,
The fate of poor mortals their pity excited :
Where Follies and Vices unite in each mind,
By Trifles diftrefs'd,---and with Baubles delighted :

To fee wretched man,
In life's narrow fpan,
Contrive to torment himfelf—all that he can ;
While none will endeavour at once to unite
The ftudy of Wifdom with Social Delight.
While none will endeavour, &c.

Then *Mercurius* addrefs'd thus the Synod around—
" A few chofen fpirits attracted my eyes,
" (As lately I travell'd o'er earth's fpacious bound)
" Who, fafhion defpifing, had dar'd to be wife :"
Father *Jove* then look'd down
From his chryftalline throne,
Which with ftar-fpangl'd luftre celeftially fhone,
To fce thofe feled, who refolv'd to unite
The ftudy of wifdom with focial delight.

Well-pleas'd with the profpect, thus fpoke mighty
Jove—
" View yon little band! link'd by Friendfhip's ftrong
" chain,
" Such merit affiftance requires from above,
" Celeftials!—Your gifts they deferve to obtain;
" Let each God beftow,
" On thofe mortals below,
" The virtues moft fuitable for them to know,
" That, improving in knowledge, they at length may
" unite
" The ftudy of wifdom with focial delight."

" My wifdom divine fhall their meetings infpire,"
Says *Minerva*, the goddefs with blue-beaming eyes,
A 2

" And I," faid *Apollo*, " I'll tune my own lyre,
" To foften their fouls, the true way to grow wife :
    " With fweet poetry,
    " United fhall be
" The ravifhing notes of divine harmony :
" Their minds in fweet unifon thus will unite
" The ftudy of wifdom with focial delight."

Says the bright fon of *Maia*, " Be eloquence mine,
" By me foft perfuafion fhall flow from each tongue ;
" And *Bacchus* will lend us a glafs of good wine."
" And, I," replied *Momus*, " the jeft and the fong."
        Thus, wine, wit, and fenfe,
        And fweet eloquence,
And mufic and fong all their charms fhall difpenfe,
A wreath to entwine, where at once will unite
The ftudy of wifdom with focial delight.

" Be it fo !" fays the thundering king of the fky,
(Whilft the cloud-cap'd *Olympus* fhudder'd with fear;)
" And when Fate cuts the thread of their life, when
    " they die,
" Son *Mercury !* you fhall conduct the lads here.
    " So each earthly gueft,
    " At our ambrofial feaft,
" Immortal fhall grow, when our nectar they tafte ;
" That, made perfect in virtue, they with us may
    " unite
" The practice of wifdom with focial delight."
    When made perfect in virtue, may we all thus unite
    The practice of wifdom with focial delight.

SONG III.

THOU SOFT FLOWING AVON.

Largetto.

Thou foft flowing Avon, by thy filver ftream,

Of things more than mortal thy Skakefpeare

would dream, would dream, would dream, thy

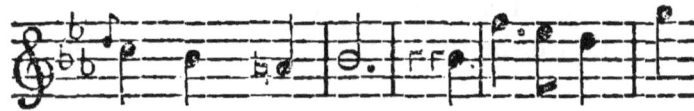

Shakefpeare would dream. The fairies, by moon-

light, dance round his green bed; For hallow'd

the turf is which pillow'd his head: The fairies,

by moonlight, dance round his green bed ; For

hallow'd the turf is which pil-low'd his head.

The love-ftricken maiden, the foft fighing fwain,
Here rove without danger, and figh without pain.
The fweet bud of beauty no blight fhall here dread ;
For hallow'd the turf is which pillow'd his head.

Here youth fhall be fam'd for their love and their
    truth,
And cheerful old age feel the fpirit of youth.
For the raptures of fancy here poets fhall tread ;
For hallow'd the turf is which pillow'd his head.

Flow on, filver Avon, in fong ever flow !
Be the fwans on thy borders ftill whiter than fnow !
Ever full be thy ftream ; like his fame may it fpread !
And the turf ever hallow'd which pillow'd his head !

SONG IV.

THE BROWN JUG.

Dear Tom, this brown jug, that now foams

with mild ale, (In which I will drink to fweet

Nan of the vale), Was once Toby Filpot, a thir-

fty old foul As e'er crack'd a bottle, or fathom'd

a bowl. In boozing a - - bout 'twas his praife

to excel, And among jol-ly topers he bore off

the bell - - - - - - - - - - - - - - - - - - he

bore off the bell.

It chanc'd as in dog-days he fat at his eafe,
In his flow'r-woven arbour as gay as you pleafe,.
With a friend and a pipe puffing forrow away,
And with honeft old ftingo was foaking his clay,
His breath-doors of life on a fudden were fhut,
And he dy'd full as big as a Dorchefter butt.

His body when long in the ground it had lain,
And time into clay had refolv'd it again,
A potter found out in its covert fo fnug,
And with part of fat Toby he form'd this brown jug.
Now, facred to friendfhip, to mirth, and mild ale;
So here's to my lovely fweet Nan of the vale.

SONG V.

ON FRIENDSHIP.

The world, my dear Myra, is full of deceit,

And friendſhip's a jewel we ſeldom can meet.

How ſtrange does it ſeem, that in ſearching a-

round, That ſource of con-tent is ſo rare to be

found! O friendſhip! thou balm and rich

ſweet'ner of life, Kind parent of eaſe, and com-po-fer of ftrife : Without thee, alas ! what are

rich-es and pow'r, But emp-ty de-lu-fion, the

joys of an hour - - - - - - - - - But emp-

ty de-lu-fion the joys of an hour.

How much to be priz'd and efteem'd is a friend
On whom we may always with fafety depend ?
Our joys, when extended, will always increafe,
And griefs, when divided, are hufh'd into peace.
When fortune is fmiling, what crowds will appear
Their kindnefs to offer, and friendfhip fincere ;
Yet change but the profpect, and point out diftrefs,
No longer to court you they eagerly prefs.

SONG VI.

WHEN ONCE THE GODS.

When once the Gods like us below, To keep

it up defign, Their goblets with frefh Nectar

flow, Which makes them more divine. Since

drinking de----fies the foul, Let's pufh a - bout

the flowing bowl, Since drinking de -- i -- fies

the foul, Let's pufh about the flowing bowl. A

B

flow - - - - - - - - - - - - ing bowl, A flow - - -

- - - - - - - - - ing bowl, fince drinking de-i-fies

the foul, Lets pufh about the flowing bowl.

The glittering ftar and ribbon blue,
   That deck the courtier's breaft,
May hide a heart of blackeft hue,
   Though by the king carefs'd.
Let him in pride and fplendour roll ;
We'er happier o'er a flowing bowl.
   A flowing bowl, &c.

For liberty let patriots rave,
   And damn the courtly crew,
Becaufe, like them, they want to have
   The loaves and fifhes too.
I care not who divides the cole,
So I can fhare a flowing bowl.
   A flowing bowl, &c.

Let Mansfield Lord-chief juftice be,
   Sir Fletcher fpeaker ftill ;

At home let Rodney rule the fea,
   And Pitt the treafury ftill :
No place I want, throughout the whole,
I want an ever-flowing bowl.
   A flowing bowl, &c. -

The fon wants fquare-toes at old Nick,
   And mifs is mad to wed ;
The doctor wants us to be fick ;
   The undertaker dead.
All have their wants from pole to pole ;
I want an ever-flowing bowl, &c.
   A flowing bowl, &c.

B 2

SONG VII.

LOCHABER NO MORE.

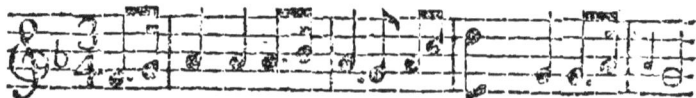

Farewell to Lochaber! and farewell, my Jean!

Where heartfome with thee I have mony days

been : For, Lochaber no more, Lochaber no

more, We'll may - be re - turn to Loch - a - ber

no more. Thefe tears that I fhed, they are

a' for my dear, And no for the dan-gers at-

tending on weir : Tho', bore on rough feas to

a far bloo - dy fhore, May - be to re - turn

to Loch - a - ber no more.

Tho' hurricanes rife, and rife ev'ry wind,
They'll ne'er make a tempeft like that in my mind :
Tho' loudeft of thunders on louder waves roar,
That's naething like leaving my love on the fhore.
To leave thee behind me my heart is fair pain'd ;
By eafe that's inglorious no fame can be gain'd :
And beauty and love's the reward of the brave ;
And I muft deferve it before I can crave.

Then glory, my Jeany, maun plead my excufe ;
Since honour commands me, how can I refufe ?
Without it I ne'er can have merit for thee,
And without thy favour I'd better not be.
I gae then, my lafs, to win honour and fame ;
And if I fhould luck to come glorioufly hame,
I'll bring a heart to thee with love running o'er,
And then I'll leave thee and Lochaber no more.

B 3

SONG VIII.

TOPSAILS SHIVER IN THE WIND.

The topfails fhi - - ver in the wind, The fhip

fhe cafts to fea; But yet my foul, my

heart, my mind, are, Ma - - ry, moor'd with

thee. For tho' thy failor's bound a--far, ftill

Love fhall be his leading ftar; For tho' thy

failor's bound a - far, Still Love fhall be his

lead - - ing ftar.

Should landmen flatter when we're fail'd,
   O doubt their artful tales ;
No gallant failor ever fail'd,
   If love breath'd conftant gales ;
Thou art the compafs of my foul
Which fteers my heart from pole to pole.

Sirens in every port we meet,
   More fell than rocks or waves :
But fuch as grace the Britifh fleet
   Are lovers and not flaves :
No foes our courage fhall fubdue,
Altho' we've left our hearts with you.

Thefe are our cares,---but if you're kind,
   We'll fcorn the dafhing main,
The rocks, the billows, and the wind,
   The power of France and Spain :
Now England's glory refts with you,
Our fails are full, fweet girls, Adieu !

SONG IX.

THE BIRKS OF INVERMAY.

The fmiling morn, the breathing fpring, In-

vite the tuneful birds to fing, And while

they warble from each fpray, Love melts the

u--ni--ver--fal lay.   Let us, A--man--da,

time---ly wife, like them improve the hour

that flies, and in foft raptures wafte the day,

a---mong the birks of In--ver--may.

For foon the winter of the year,
And age, life's winter, will appear,
At this thy living bloom will fade,
As that will ftrip thy verdant fhade;
Our tafte of pleafure then is o'er,
The feather'd fongfters are no more;
And when they droop, and we decay,
Adieu the birks of Invermay.

Behold the hills and vales around,
With lowing herds and flocks abound;
The wanton kids and frifking lambs,
Gambol and dance about their dams;
The bufy bees with humming noife,
And all the reptile kind rejoice;
Let us like them, then fing and play
About the birks of Invermay.

Hark, how the waters as they fall,
Loudly my love to gladnefs call:
The wanton waves fport in the beams,
And fifhes play throughout the ftreams;
The circling fun does now advance,
And all the planets round him dance:
Let us as jovial be as they
Among the birks of Invermay.

SONG X.

THE LAND OF DELIGHT.

As you mean to set sail for the land of de-

light, And in wedlock's soft hammock to

swing every night: If you hope that your

voyage suc--cefs-ful shou'd prove, Fill your sails

with affection, your cabins with love. If you

hope that your voyage succefsful should prove.

Fill your fails with affection, your cabins with

love. Fill your fails with affection, your

ca-bins with love.

Let your heart, like the main-maft, be ever upright,
And the union you boaft, like our tackle, be tight;
Of the fhoals of indiff'rence be fure to keep clear,
And the quickfands of jealoufy never come near.

But if vapours and whims, like fea-ficknefs prevail,
You muft fpread all your canvas and catch the frefh
gale.   [fea,
For if brifk blows the wind, and there comes a rough
You muft lower your top-fail, and fcud under lee.

If hufbands e'er hope to live peaceable lives,
They muft reckon themfelves, give the helm to their
wives:
For the fmoother we fail, boys, we're fafeft from
harm,
And on fhipboard the head is ftill rul'd by the helm.

Then lift to your pilot, my boys, and be wife;
If my precepts you fcorn, and my maxims defpife,
A brace of proud antlers your brows may adorn;
And a hundred to one but you double Cape Horn.

SONG XI.

QUEEN MARY'S LAMENTATION.

I figh and lament me in vain, Thefe walls

can but e-----cho my moan, A—las,   it en-

creafes   my   pain,   When I think   of the

days that are   gone : Thro' the grate of my

prifon, I fee the birds as they wanton in
air, My heart how it pants to be free, My
looks they are wild with de————fpair.

Above tho' oppreft by my fate,
　I burn with contempt for my foes,
Tho' fortune has alter'd my ftate,
　She ne'er can fubdue me to thofe.
Falfe woman ! in ages to come
　Thy malice detefted fhall be ;
And when we are cold in the tomb
　Some heart ftill will forrow for me.

Ye roofs where cold damps and difmay,
　With filence and folitude dwell,
How comfortlefs paffes the day,
　How fad tolls the evening bell ;
The owls from the battlements cry,
　Hollow wind feems to murmur around,
" O Mary, prepare thee to die,"
　My blood it runs cold at the found.

C

SONG XII.

ETRICK BANKS.

On E-trick banks, ae fummer's night, At

gloming when the fheep drave hame, I met

my laffie braw and tight, Came wading bare-

foot a' her lane: My heart grew light, I

ran, I flang My arms about her li---ly

neck, And kifs'd and clapp'd her there fu'

lang, My words they were na mon—y feck.

I faid, My laſſie, will ye go
  To the Highland hills, the Earſe to learn,
I'll baith gi'e thee a cow and ew,
  When ye come to the brig of Earn.
At Leith auld meal comes in, ne'er faſh,
  And herring at the Broomielaw;
Cheer up your heart, my bonny laſs,
  There's gear to win we never faw.

All day when we have wrought eneugh,
  When winter, froſt and ſnaw begin,
Soon as the ſun gaes weſt the loch,
  At night when ye ſit down to ſpin,
I'll ſcrew my pipes and play a ſpring:
  And thus the weary night we'll end,
Till the tender kid and lamb-time bring
  Our pleaſant ſummer back again.

Syne when the trees are in their bloom,
  And gowans glent o'er ilka field,
I'll meet my laſs amang the broom,
  And lead you to my ſummer ſheild.
Then far frae a' their ſcornfu' din,
  That make the kindly hearts their ſport,
We'll laugh and kiſs, and dance and ſing,
  And gar the langeſt day ſeem ſhort.

C 2

SONG XIII.

LET'S SEEK THE BOWER.

Let's feek the bower of Robinhood, This is

his bridal day, And cheerfully in blythe Sher-

wood, bridemaids and bridemen play.   Then

follow, follow me, my bonny, bonny lads, And

we'll the paftime fee; For the minftrels fing,

And the fweet bells ring,   And they feaft right

merrily, merrily; And they feaft right mer-

rily, mer-ri-ly.

The humming beer flows round in pails,
  With mead that's ftoud and old,
And am'rous virgins tell love-tales,
  To thaw the heart that's cold.
Then follow me, my bonny lads,
  And we'll the paftime fee ;
    For the minftrels fing,
    And the fweet bells ring,
And they feaft right merrily.

There, dancing fprightly on the green,
  Each lightfoot lad and lafs,
Sly ftealing kiffes when unfeen,
  And gingling glafs with glafs.
Then follow me, my bonny lads,
  And we'll the paftime fee ;
    For the minftrels fing,
    And the fweet bells ring,
And they feaft right merrily.

C 3

SONG XIV.

HOW SWEET THE LOVE.

When firſt I ken'd young Sandie's face, He

ſung and look'd wi' ſic a grace, He ſung

and look'd wi' ſic a grace, He ſtole my

heart, but did na care; The lad he

lo'ed a laſs more fair: And oft I ſung o'er

brae and burn, How ſweet's the love that

meets return.

He lo'ed a lafs wi' fickle mind,
Was fometimes cauld and fometimes kind ;
Which made the love-fick laddie rue ;
For fhe was cauld when he was true ;
He mourn'd and fung, o'er brae and burn,
How fweet's the love that meets return.

One day a pretty wreath he twin'd,
Where lilacks with fweet cowflips join'd,
To make a garland for her hair ;
But fhe refus'd the gift fo fair.
This fcorn, he cry'd, can ne'er be borne ;
But fweet's the love that meets return.

Juft then he met my tell-tale een,
And love fo true is fooneft feen :
Dear lafs, faid he, my heart is thine ;
For thy foft wifhes are like mine :
Now Jenny, in her turn, may mourn,
How fweet's the love that meets return !

My anfwer was both frank and kind ;
I lo'ed the lad, and tell'd my mind :
To kirk we went wi' hearty glee,
And wha fae bleft as he and me !
Now blithe we fing, o'er brae and burn,
How fweet's the love that meets return !

SONG XV.

WHAT CARE I HOW FAIR SHE BE.

Allegretto.

Shall I, wafting in defpair, Die becaufe a

woman's fair? Shall my cheeks look pale with

care, 'Caufe another's rofy are? Shall my cheeks

look pale with care, 'Caufe a--nother's ro--fy

are? Caufe a-nother's ro - fy are? Be fhe fairer

than the day, Or the flowery meads in May;

Yet, if she think not well of me, What care I

how fair she be? Be she fairer than the day, Or

the flowery meads in May, Yet, if she think not

well of me, What care I how fair she be? What

care I? What care I? What care I how fair she

be? But if she think not well of me, What care I

how fair she be? What care I how fair she be?

Shall a woman's goodnefs move
Me to perifh for her love ?
Or, her worthy merits known,
Make me quite forget my own ?
Be fhe with that goodnefs bleft
As may merit name the beft ;
Yet if fhe be not fuch to me,
What care I how good fhe be ?

Be fhe good, or kind, or fair,
I will never more defpair ;
If fhe love me, this believe,
I will die 'ere fhe fhall grieve ;
If fhe flight me when I woo,
I will fcorn and let her go,
So if fhe be not fit for me,
What care I for whom fhe be ?

SONG XVI.

CORN RIGS.

My Patie is a lo--ver gay, His mind is ne-

ver muddy, His breath is fweeter than new

hay, His face is fair and rud---dy. His fhape

is handfome, mid - dle fize, He's comely in

his wa'k--ing, The fhining of his een fur-

prife, 'Tis heaven to hear him ta'k - ing.

Laſt night I met him on a bawk,
    Where yellow corn was growing :
There mony a kindly word he ſpake,
    That ſet my heart a-glowing.
He kifs'd, and vow'd he wad be mine,
    And loo'd me beſt of ony ;
That gars me like to ſing ſinſyne,
    O corn-rigs are bonny !

Let laſſes of a ſilly mind
    Refuſe what maiſt they're wanting ?
Since we for yielding we're deſign'd,
    We chaſtly ſhould be granting.
Then I'll comply and marry PATE ;
    And fyne my cockernony
He's free to touzel air or late,
    Where corn-rigs are bonny.

SONG XVII.

Tune---" CORN RIGS ARE BONNY."

LORD! what care I for mam or dad!
Why, let them fcold and bellow;
For while I live I'll love my lad,
He's fuch a charming fellow.
The laft fair day, on yonder green,
The youth he danc'd fo well, O;
So fpruce a lad was never feen
As my fweet charming fellow.

The fair was o'er, and night was come,
The lad was fomewhat mellow;
Says he, my dear, I'll fee you home;
I thank'd the charming fellow.
We trudg'd along, the moon fhone bright;
Says he, my fweeteft Nell, O,
I'll kifs you here by this good light;
Lord, what a charming fellow!

You rogue, fays I, you've ftopp'd my breath;
Ye bells ring out my knell, O;
Again I'd die fo fweet a death
With fuch a charming fellow.
You rogue, fays I, you've ftopp'd my breath;
Ye bells ring out my knell, O;
Again I'd die fo fweet a death
With fuch a charming fellow!

D

SONG XVIII.

THE WANDERING SAILOR.

The wand'ring fail-or ploughs the main, A

com-pe-tence in life to gain; Undaunted

braves the ftormy feas, To find at laft content

and eafe ; To find at laft content and eafe : In

hopes when toil and danger's o'er, To an-chor

on his native fhore ; In hopes when toil and

danger's o'er, To anchor on his na-tive fhore,

To anchor on his native fhore. When winds

blow hard, and mountains roll, And thunders

fhake from pole to pole ; Tho' dreadful waves

furrounding foam, Still flatt'ring fan-cy wafts

him home, Still flatt'ring fan - cy wafts him home,

In hopes, when toil and danger's o'er, To an-

chor on his native fhore; In hopes, when toil

and danger's o'er, To anchor on his na - - tive

fhore; To anchor on his native fhore.

* When round the bowl the jovial crew
The early fcenes of youth renew,
'Tho' each his fav'rite fair will boaft,
This is the univerfal toaft :
This is the univerfal toaft :
 May we, when toil and danger's o'er,
 Caft anchor on our native fhore !
 May we, when toil and danger's o'er,
 Caft anchor on our native fhore !
 Caft anchor on our native fhore !

 * Thefe words to be fung to the firft part of the tune.

SONG XIX.

BLOW HIGH, BLOW LOW.

Blow high, blow low, let tempests tear the

mainmaft by the board, My heart, with thoughts

of thee, my dear, and love well ftor'd, Shall

brave all danger, Scorn all fear, The roaring

winds, the raging fea, In hopes on fhore To be

once more Safe moor'd with thee.   A--loft

while mountains high we go, The whiffling

winds that fcud a - long, And the furge roaring

from below, Shall my fignal be to think on thee,

Shall my fignal be to think on thee ;

And this fhall be my fong : And on that night

when all the crew the mem'ry of their former

lives O'er flowing canns of flip renew, and drink

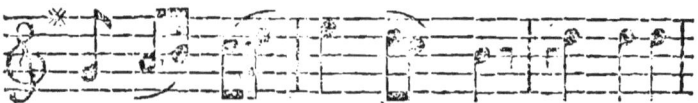

their fweethearts and their wives, I'll heave a

figh, I'll heave a figh, and think on thee ; And

as the fhip rolls thro' the fea, The burden of my

Da Capo.

fong fhall be :

SONG XX.

ROSLIN CASTLE.

'Twas in that feafon of the year, When all

things gay and fweet appear, That Colin, with

the morning ray, A--rofe and fung his ru--ral

lay. Of Nanny's charms the fhepherd fung,

The hills and dales with Nan - ny rung, While

Roflin caftle heard the fwain, And e - cho'd

tr.

back the cheerful ftrain,

Awake, fweet mufe ! the breathing fpring
With rapture warns ; awake and fing !
Awake and join the vocal throng
Who hail the morning with a fong !
To Nanny raife the chearful lay ;
O bid her hafte and come away ;
In fweeteft fmiles herfelf adorn,
And add new graces to the morn.

O hark, my love ! on ev'ry fpray
Each feather'd warbler tunes his lay !
'Tis beauty fires the ravifh'd fong,
And love infpires-the melting throng.
Then let my raptur'd notes arife :
For beauty darts from Nanny's eyes ;
And love my rifing bofom warms,
And fills my foul with fweet alarms.

O come, my love ! thy Colin's lay
With rapture calls ; O come away !
Come, while the mufe this wreath fhall twine
Around that modeft brow of thine !
O hither hafte, and with thee bring
That beauty blooming like the fpring !
Thofe graces that divinely fhine !
And charm this ravifh'd breaft of mine.

SONG XXI.

To the foregoing Tune.

From Roflin Caftle's echoing walls
Refounds my fhepherd's ardent calls;
My Colin bids me come away,
And love demands I fhould obey.
His melting ftrain and tuneful lay
So much the charms of love difplay,
I yield,—nor longer can refrain
To own my love, and blefs my fwain.

No longer can my heart conceal
The painful pleafing flame I feel;
My foul retorts the am'rous ftrain,
And echoes back in love again.
Where lurks my fongfter? From what grove
Does Colin pour his notes of love?
O bring me to the happy bow'r
Where mutual love may blifs fecure!

Ye vocal hills that catch the fong,
Repeating, as it flies along,
To Colin's ear my ftrain convey,
And fay, I hafte to come away.
Ye zephyrs foft that fan the gale,
Waft to my love the foothing tale;
In whifpers all my foul exprefs,
And tell, I hafte his arms to blefs.

SONG XXII.

THE HIGH-METTLED RACER.

See the courfe throng'd with gazers, the fports

are begun; The con - fu - fion, but hear, I bet

you, Sir! Done! done! Ten thoufand ftrange

murmurs refound far and near, Lords, hawk-

ers and jockies, affail the tir'd ear; Lords,

hawkers, and jockies, affail the tir'd ear. While

with neck like a rainbow, erecting his creft,

Pamper'd, prancing, and pleas'd, his head

touching his breaft ; Scarcely fnuff--ing the air,

he's fo proud and e - late, The high-mettled

ra - - cer firft ftarts for the plate ; The high-

mettled ra - - cer, The high-mettled racer

firft ftarts for the plate.

Grown aged, us'd up, and turn'd out of the ftud,
Lame, fpavin'd, and wind-gall'd ; but yet with fome
   blood :
While knowing poftilions his pedigree trace,
Tell his dam won that fweep, his fire that race ;

And what matches he won to the hoftlers count o'er
As they loiter their time at fome hedge ale-houfe door,
While the harnefs fore galls, and the fpurs his fides
    goad,
The high-mettled racer's a hack on the road.

Till at laft, having labour'd, drudg'd early and late,
Bow'd down, by degrees he bends on to his fate ;
Blind, old, lean, and feeble, he tugs round a mill,
Or draws fand till the fand of his hour-glafs ftands ftill:
And now, cold and lifelefs, expos'd to the view
In the very fame cart which he yefterday drew ;
While a pitying crowd his fad relics furrounds,
The high-mettled racer is fold for the hounds.

E

SONG XXIII.

KISS THE COLD WINTER AWAY.

Hey for a lafs and a bottle to cheer, And a

thumping bantling every year; Hey for a lafs

and a bottle to cheer, And a thumping bantling

e-ve-ry year. With fkin as white as fnow, And

hair as brown as a berry; With eyes as

black as a floe, And lips as red as a cher-ry.

With fkin as white as fnow, And hair as brown

as a berry; With eyes as black as a floe, And

lips as red as a cherry. Sing rouly, toufy, ran-

tum, fcantum, Laugh and lie down is the play:

We'll cuddle together, To keep out the weather,

And kifs the cold winter away; Kifs, kifs

the cold winter away, Kifs, kifs the cold

win-ter a - way.

Laugh while you live;
For, as life is a jeft,
Who laughs the moft,
Is fure to live beft.

E 2

When I was not fo old,
I frolick'd among the miffes ;
And, when they thought me too bold,
I ftopp'd their mouths with kiffes.
Sing roufy, toufy, &c.

SONG XXIV.

THE YELLOW HAIR'D LADDIE.

In April, when Primrofes paint the fweet

plain, And fummer ap-proach-ing re---joi--ceth

the fwain. joiceth the fwain, The yellow-hair'd

laddie would of-ten-times go, To wilds and

deep glens where the hawthorn trees grow.

hawthorn trees grow.

There, under the fhade of an old facred thorn,
With freedom he fung his loves evening and morn,
He fang with fo foft and enchanting a found,
That Sylvans and fairies unfeen danc'd around.

The fhepherd thus fung : Tho' young Maddie be fair
Her beauty is dafh'd with a fcornful proud air :
But Sufie was handfome, and fweetly could fing ;
Her breath, like the breezes, perfum'd in the fpring.

That Maddie, in all the gay bloom of her youth,
Like the moon, was inconftant, and never fpoke truth:
But Sufie was faithful, good-humour'd, and free,
And fair as the goddefs that fprung from the fea.

That mamma's fine daughter, with all her great
    dow'r,
Was aukwardly airy, and frequently four :
Then, fighing, he wifh'd, would parents agree,
The witty, fweet Sufan, his miftrefs might be.

E 3

SONG XXV.

MY TRIM-BUILT WHERRY.

Then farewell, my trim-built wherry, Oars,

and coat and badge, farewell; Never more at

Chelfea fer-ry Shall your Thomas take a fpell.

Then farewell, my trim-built wherry, Oars,

and coat and badge, farewell; Never more at

Chelfea fer - - ry fhall your Thomas take a

fpell - -; Shall your Tho - mas take a fpell.

But, to hope and peace a stranger,
  In the battle's heat I go ;
Where, expos'd to every danger,
  Some friendly ball may lay me low.

Then, mayhap, when homeward steering,
  With the news my messmates come ;
Even you, my story hearing,
  With a sigh may cry—" poor Tom."

SONG XXVI.

FOR ME MY FAIR.

For me my fair a wreath has wove, Where rival

flow'rs in union meet, Where rival flow'rs in

union meet : As oft fhe kifs'd this gift of love,

Her breath gave fweetnefs to the fweet ; As

oft fhe kifs'd this gift of love, Her breath gave

fweetnefs to the fweet, Her breath gave fweet-

nefs to the fweet.

A bee within a damaſk roſe
  Had crept, the nectar'd dew to ſip ;
But leſſer ſweets the thief foregoes,
  And fixes on Louiſa's lip.

There, taſting all the bloom of ſpring,
  Wak'd by the ripening breath of May,
Th' ungrateful ſpoiler left his ſting,
  And with the honey fled away.

SONG XXVII.

THE BANKS OF FORTH.

Ye Syl-vi-an pow'rs that rule the plain,

where sweetly wind - ing Forth - - a glides, Con-

duct me to her banks a - - - gain, Since there

my charming Ma----ry bides. These banks that

breathe their ver-nal sweets Where ev'--ry smil-ing

beau------ty meets, where Mary's charms a-dorn the

plain, And chear the heart of ev'-------ry swain,

Oft in the thick embow'ring groves,
   Where birds their mufic chirp aloud,
Alternately they fing their loves,
   And Fortha's fair meanders view'd.
The meadows wore a general fmile,
Love was our banquet all the while ;
The lovely profpect charm'd the eye,
To where the ocean met the fky.

Once on the graffy bank reclin'd,
   Where Forth ran by in murmurs deep,
It was my happy chance to find
   The charming Mary lull'd afleep.
My heart then leap'd with inward blifs,
I foftly ftoop'd and ftole a kifs ;
She wak'd, fhe blufh'd, and gently blam'd,
" Why, Damon ! are you not afham'd ?"

Ye fylvan Powers, ye Rural Gods,
   To whom we fwains our cares impart,
Reftore me to thefe blefs'd abodes,
   And eafe, oh ! eafe my love-fick heart :
Thefe happy days again reftore,
When Mall and I fhall part no more ;
When fhe fhall fill thefe longing arms,
And crown my blifs with all her charms.

SONG XXVIII.

THE BLUSH OF AURORA.

The blufh of Au—ro—ra now tinges the morn,

And dew-drops be—-fpangle the fweet fcented

thorn ; Then found bro—-ther fportfman, found

found the gay horn, Till Phœbus a—--wakens the

day, Till Phœ--bus a—--wa—kens the day :

And fee now he ri--fes ! in fplendor how

Sym.   Sym.

bright ! I O Pe an ! I O Pe an !

for Phœbus, for Phœbus the god of de-light, All

glorious in beauty now ba--nifh--es night : Then

mount, boys, to horfe and away, To horfe and

a - - way, to horfe and away, a - - way - - - - -

- - - - - - - - - - - - - - Then mount boys, then

F

mount boys, then mount boys, then mount boys,

then mount boys, to horfe and away.

What raptures can equal the joys of the chace !
Health, bloom, aud contentment appear in each face,
And in our fwift courfers what beauty and grace,
 While we the fleet ftag do purfue ;
 While we. &c.
At the deep and harmonious fweet cry of the hounds,
Wing'd by terror, wing'd by terror,   [bounds,
Wing'd by terror, he burfts from the foreft's wide
And tho' like the light'ning he darts o'er the grounds,
 Yet ftill, boys, we keep him in view.
We keep him in view, we keep him in view, in view,
And tho' like the light'ning, &c.

When chac'd till quite fpent, he his life does refign,
Our victim we'll offer at Bacchus's fhrine ;
And revel in honour of Nimrod divine,
 That hunter fo mighty of fame.
 That hunter, &c.
Our glaffes then charge to our country and king,

Love and beauty; love and beauty;
Love and beauty we'll fill to, and jovially fing;
Wifhing health and fuccefs, till we make the houfe
  ring,
  To all fportfmen and fons of the game.
And fons of the game; and fons of the game; the
  game;
Wifhing health and fuccefs, &c.

SONG XXIX:

BY THE GAILY CIRCLING GLASS.

By the gaily circling glafs, We· can fee how

minutes pafs; By the hollow cafk we're told How

the waning night grows old, How the waning

night grows old. Soon, too foon, the bu-

fy day drives as from our fport a--

way. What have we with day to do ? Sons

of Care, 'twas made for you ! Sons of Care,

'twas made for you!

By the filence of the owl,
  By the chirping on the thorn,
By the butts that empty roll,
  We foretel th' approach of morn,
Fill, then, fill the vacant glafs,
  Let no precious moment flip ;
Flout the moralizing afs ;
  Joys find entrance at the lip.

F 3

SONG XXX.

BRAES OF BALLENDEAN.

Be - neath a green fhade a lovely young

fwain, one ev'ning re-clin'd to dif---co-----ver

his pain: So fad, yet fo fweetly, he

warbled his woe, The wind ceas'd to breathe,

And the foun---tains to flow; Rude winds

with compaffion could hear him complain, yet

Chloe lefs gentle was deaf to his ftrain.

How happy, he cry'd, my moments once flew,
E'er Chloe's bright charms firft flafh'd on my view !
Thofe eyes, then, with pleafure, the dawn could fur-
   vey,
Nor fmil'd the fair morning more chearful than they,
Now fcenes of diftrefs pleafe only my fight,
I ficken in pleafure, and languifh in light.

Thro' changes, in vain, relief I purfue :
All, all, but confpire, my griefs to renew :
From funfhine, to zephyrs and fhades we repair ;
To funfhine we fly from too piercing an air :
But love's ardent fever burns always the fame !
No winter can cool it, no fummer inflame.

But, fee ! the pale moon, all clouded, retires !
The breezes grow cool, not Strephon's defires !
I fly from the dangers of tempeft and wind :
Yet nourifh the madnefs that preys on my mind.
Ah, wretch ! how can life be worthy thy care,
Since length'ning it's moments but lengthens de-
   fpair.

SONG XXXI.

TO THE GREENWOOD GANG WI' ME.

To fpeer my love, wi' glances fair, The

woodland lad-die came ; He vow'd he wou'd be

ay fin-cere, And thus he fpake his flame : The

morn is blithe, my bon - ny fair, As blithe as

blithe can be ; To the green wood gang, my

laffie dear, To the green wood gang wi' me,

Gang wi' me, gang wi' me, To the green

wood gang, my laffie dear, To the green

wood gang wi' me.

The lad wi' love was fo opprefs'd,
   I wad na fay him nay;
My lips he kifs'd, my hand he prefs'd,
   While tripping o'er the brae :
Dear lad, I cry'd, thou'rt trig and fair,
   And blithe as blithe can be ;
To the green wood gang, my laddie dear,
   To the green wood gang wi' me.

The bridal day is come to pafs,
   Sic joy was never feen ;
Now I am call'd the woodland lafs,
   The woodland laddie's queen :
I blefs the morn fo frefh and fair
   I told my mind fo free,
" To the green wood gang, my laddie dear,
   " To the green wood gang wi' me."

SONG XXXII.

BRIGHT PHOEBUS.

Bright Phœbus has mounted the chariot of day,

And the horns and the hounds call each fportf-

man a - way ; And the horns and the hounds call

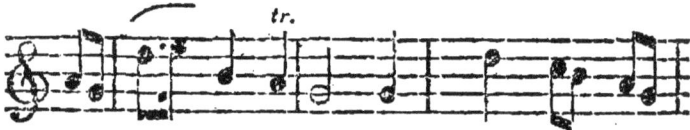

each fportfman away. Thro' woods and thro'

meadows with fpeed now they bound, While

health, ro - fy health, is in ex - er - cife found ;

Thro' woods and thro' meadows with fpeed now

they bound, While health, rofy health, is in

tr.

ex - er - cife found. Hark away! Hark a-

way! Hark away is the word to the found

of the horn - - - - - - - - - - - - - - - -

- - - - - - - - - - - - - - And e - cho and

e - - cho, And e - - cho, blithe e - cho, makes

jo--vial the morn.

Each hill and each valley is lovely to view,
While pufs flies the covert, and dogs quick purfue.
Behold where fhe flies o'er the wide-fpreading plain !
While the loud op'ning pack purfue her amain.
    Hark away, &c.

At length pufs is caught, and lies panting for breath,
And the fhout of the huntfman's the fignal for death.
No joys can delight like the fports of the field ;
To hunting all pleafures and paftimes muft yield.
    Hark away, &c.

SONG XXXIII.

THO' LEIXLIP IS PROUD.

Tho' Leixlip is   proud of its clofe fhady bowers

Its clear-fall---ing waters, its murm'ring cafcades,

Its groves of fine myrtle, its beds of sweet flowers,

Its lads so well dress'd, and its neat pretty maids :

As each his own village will still make the most of,

In praise of dear Carton I hope I'm not wrong,

Dear Carton containing what kingdoms may boast of,

'Tis Norah, dear Norah, the theme of my song. Dear

Carton, containing what kingdoms may boast of,

G

'Tis Norah, dear Norah, the theme of my fong.

Be gentlemen fine, with their fpurs and nice boots on,
    Their horfes to ftart on the Curragh of Kildare,
Or dance at a ball with their Sunday new fuits on,
    Lac'd waiftcoat, white gloves, and their nice pow-
        der'd hair :
Poor Pat, while fo bleft in his mean humble ftation,
    For gold, or for acres, he never fhall long.
One fweet fmile can give him the wealth of a nation,
    From Norah, dear Norah, the theme of my fong.

SONG XXXIV.

SAE MERRY AS WE TWA HAE BEEN.

Slow.

A lafs that was laden with care fat hea-vi- ly

under yon thorn, I liften'd a while for to hear,

When thus fhe be - gan for to mourn : Whene'er

my dear fhepherd was here, The birds did melo-

dioufly fing, And cold nipping winter did wear A

face that refembled the fpring. Sae merry as

we twa hae been ; Sae merry as we twa hae been;

My heart it is like for to break when I think

on the days we have feen.

G 2

Our flocks feeding clofe by his fide,
   He gently prefling my hand,
I view'd the wide world in its pride,
   And laugh'd at the pomp of command !
" My dear," he wou'd oft to me fay,
   " What makes you hard-hearted to me ?
" Oh ! why do you thus turn away
   " From him who is dying for thee !
      Sae merry, &c.
But now he is far from my fight,
   And perhaps a deceiver may prove ;
Which makes me lament day and night,
   That ever I granted my love.
At eve, when the reft of the folk
   Are merrily feated to fpin,
I fet myfelf under an oak,
   And heavily figh for him.
      Sae merry, &c.

SONG XXXV.
MAY EVE : OR, KATE OF ABERDEEN.

The filver moon's en - a - mour'd beam

Steals foft - ly through the night. To wanton

with the wind - ing ftream, And kifs re - flect -

ed light. To beds of ftate go, balm - y fleep,

('Tis where you've feldom been), May's vi - gil

while the fhep-herds keep with Kate of A - ber-

deen, With Kate of A - ber - deen, with Kate

of A - - ber - - deen.

Upon the green the virgins wait,
In rofy chaplets gay,

G 3

Till morn unbar her golden gate,
And give the promis'd May.
Methinks I hear the maids declare
The promis'd May, when feen,
Not half fo fragrant, half fo fair,
As Kate of Aberdeen.

SONG XXXVI.

COME, COME MY JOLLY LADS.

Come, come, my jolly lads, the wind's abaft, brifk

gales our fails fhall crowd ; Come buftle, buftle

buftle boys, Hawl the boat, the boatfwain pipes

a-loud. The fhip's unmoor'd, All hands on board,

The rifing gale fills ev'ry fail, The fhip's well

mann'd and ftor'd : Then fling the flowing bowl ;

Fond hopes arife, The girls we prize Shall blefs

each jovial foul. The cann, boys, bring, we'll drink

and fing, while foaming billows roll.

Tho' to the Spanifh coaft
    We're bound to fteer,
We'll ftill our rights maintain;
Then bear a hand, be fteady, boys,
    Soon we'll fee
Old England once again :
    From fhore to fhore,
    While cannons roar,

Our tars fhall fhew
The haughty foe
   Britannia rules the main.

Then fling the flowing bowl;
Fond hopes arife,
The girls we prize
Shall blefs each jovial foul:
   The cann, boys, bring,
   We'll drink and fing,
While foaming billows roll.

Cho.   Then fling the, *&c.*

SONG XXXVII.

THE BRAES OF YARROW.

The fun juft glancing through the trees,

gave light and joy to ilk - a grove, And plea-

fure in each fouthern breeze A-wak-en'd hope

and flumb'ring love. When Jen--ny fung with

hear-ty glee, to charm her win-fome marrow

My bon-ny laddie, gang wi' me, My bon - ny

lad‑die gang wi' me, We'll o'er the braes of‑

Yarrow: My bonny laddie, gang wi' me,

We'll o'er the braes of Yarrow, We'll o'er

the braes of Yarrow, We'll o'er the braes

of Yarrow, My bonny lad‑die gang wi'

me, We'll oe'r the braes of Yarrow.

'Young Sandy was the blytheſt ſwain
That ever pip'd on bonny brae ;
Nae laſs could ken him free frae pain,
Sae graceful, kind, ſae fair and gay.
    And Jenny ſung, &c.

He kiſs'd and lov'd the bonny maid,
Her ſparkling e'en had won his heart,
No laſs the youth had e'er betray'd :
No fear had ſhe, the lad no art.
    And Jenny ſung, &c.

SONG XXXVIII.

THE LAST TIME I CAME OE'R THE MOOR.

The laſt time I came o'er the muir, I left my

love behind me : Ye pow'rs what pain do I

endure, when ſoft i -- de - as mind me. Soon

as the ruddy morn diſplay'd, the beaming day

en-fu-ing, I met betimes my love - ly maid

In fit re -- treats for woo - ing.

Beneath the cooling ſhade we lay,
Gazing and chaſtely ſporting ;

We kifs'd and promis'd time away,
   'Till night fpread her black curtain.
I pitied all beneath the fkies,
   Even kings when fhe was nigh me ;
In raptures I beheld her eyes,
   Which could but ill deny me.

Should I be call'd where cannons roar,
   Where mortal fteel may wound me ;
Or caft upon fome foreign fhore,
   Where dangers may furround me ;
Yet hopes again to fee my love,
   To feaft on glowing kiffes,
Shall make my care at diftance move,
   In profpect of fuch bliffes.

In all my foul there's not one place
   To let a rival enter ;
Since fhe excels in every grace,
   In her my love fhall center.
Sooner the feas fhall ceafe to flow,
   Their waves the Alps to cover ;
On Greenland's ice fhall rofes grow,
   Before I ceafe to love her.

The next time I gang o'er the muir,
   She fhall a lover find me ;
And that my faith is firm and pure,
   Tho' I left her behind me.
Then Hymen's facred bonds fhall chain
   My heart to her fair bofom ;
There, while my being does remain,
   My love more frefh fhall bloffom.

† H

SONG XXXIX.

TALLY HO.

Ye fportfmen draw near, and ye fportfwomen

too, Who delight in the joys of the field, Who

delight in the joys of the field. Mankind, tho' they

blame, are all eager as you, And no one the

conteft will yield, --- And no one the conteft

will yield. His Lordfhip, his worfhip, his ho-

nour, his grace, a-hunting con - - ti - nual - ly

go, All ranks and degrees are engag'd in the

chace, With hark forward, huzza, tally ho, - - -

- - All ranks and degrees are engag'd in the

chace, Hark forward, huzza, tally ho, - - - tally

ho, tally ho, tally ho, tally ho, tally ho, tally

ho, tally ho, - - - - hark forward, huzza

tal-ly ho - - - - - - - ..

The lawyer will rife with the firft of the morn
　To hunt for a mortgage or deed ;
The hufband gets up at the found of the horn
　Anc rides to the commons full fpeed ;
The patriot is thrown in purfuit of the game ;
　The poet too often lays low,
Who, mounted on Pegafus, flies after fame,
　With hark forward, huzza, tally ho.

While fearlefs o'er hills and o'er woodlands we fweep
　Tho' prudes on our paftime may frown,
How oft do they Decency's bounds overleap
　And the fences of Virtue break down ?
Thus public, or private, for penfion, for place,
　For amufement, for paffion, for fhew,
All ranks and degrees are engag'd in the chace,
　With hark forward, huzza, tally ho.

SONG XL.

I'LL NEVER LEAVE THEE.

One day I heard Mary fay, How fhall I leave

thee ? Stay, deareft A - - donis, ftay, Why

wilt thou grieve me ?   Alas, my fond heart.

will break, If thou fhould leave me ! I'll live

and die for thy fake, Yet never leave thee.

Say, lovely Adonis, fay,
    Has Mary deceiv'd thee ?
Did e'er her young heart betray,
    New love to grieve thee ?

H 3

My conftant mind ne'er fhall ftray,
Thou may believe me ;
I'll love thee, lad, night and day,
And never leave thee.

Adonis, my charming youth,
What can relieve thee ?
Can Mary thy anguifh foothe,
This breaft fhall receive thee.
My paffion can ne'er decay,
Never deceive thee :
Delight fhall drive pain away,
Pleafure revive thee.

But leave thee, lad, leave thee, lad,
How fhall I leave thee ?
O ! that thought makes me fad ?
I'll never leave thee.
Where would my Adonis fly ?
Why does he grieve me ?
Alas ! my poor heart will die,
If I fhould leave thee.

SONG XLI.

CONTENTED I AM.

Contented I am, and con-tent-ed I'll be, Re-

folv'd in this life to live happy and free. With

the cares of this world I'm feldom perplex'd;

I'm fometimes un--ea--fy, but never am vex'd,.

Some higher, fome lower, I own there may

be; But there's more who live worfe than live

better than me.

My life is a compound of freedom and eafe ;
I go where I will, and return when I pleafe ;
I live above envy, alfo above ftrife ;
And wifh I had judgment to choofe a good wife :
I'm neither fo high nor fo low in degree,
But ambition and want are both ftrangers to me.

Did you know how delightful my gay hours do pafs,
With my bottle before me, embrac'd by my lafs ;
I'm happy while with her, contented alone ;
My wine is my kingdom ; my cafk is my throne ;
My glafs is the fceptre by which I fhall reign :
And my whole privy council's a flafk of Champaign.

When money comes in, I live well till it's gone ;
While I have it quite happy, contented with none.
If I lofe it at gaming, I think it but lent ;
If I fpend it genteelly, I'm always content,
Thus in mirth and good humour my gay hours do pafs,
And on Saturday's night I am juft as I was.

SONG XLII.

THE TOBACCO-BOX. A Dialogue.

Thomas.

Tho' the fate of battle on to - mor - row

wait, Let's not lofe our prattle, now, my

charm - - - ing Kate, 'I ill the hour of glory,

love fhould now take place ; Nor damp the joys

before you with a fu - - - - - - ture cafe.

Kate. Oh, my Thomas, ftill be conftant, ftill be true !
Be but to your Kate, as Kate is ftill to you ;
Glory will attend you, ftill will make us bleft ;
With my firmeft love, my dear you're ftill poffeft.

Tho. No new beauties tafted, I'm their arts above;
Three campaigns are wafted, but not fo my love;
Anxious ftill about thee, thou art all I prize ;
Never, Kate without thee, will I bung thefe
eyes.

Kate. Conftant to my Thomas I will ftill remain,
Nor think I will leave thy fide the whole cam-
paign;
But I'll cherifh thee, and ftrive to make thee bold:
May'ft thou fhare the victory ! may'ft thou
fhare the gold !

Tho. If, by fome bold action, I the halbert bear,
Think what fatisfaction, when my rank you
fhare.
Drefs'd like any lady-fair from top to toe ;
Fine lac'd caps and ruffles then will be your due.

Kate. If a ferjeant's lady l fhould chance to prove,
Linen fhall be ready always for my love;
Never more will Kate the captain's laundrefs
be :
I'm too pretty, Thomas, love, for all but thee.

Tho. Here, Kate, take my 'bacco-box, a foldier's all ;
If by Frenchmens blows your Tom is doom'd
to fall,
When my life is ended, thou may'ft boaft and
prove,
Thou'd'ft my firft, my laft, my only pledge of
love.

Kate. Here, take back thy 'bacco-box, thou'rt all to me;
Nor think but I will be near thee, love, to fee;
In the hour of danger let me always fhare;
I'll be kept no ftranger to my foldier's fare.

Tho. Check that rifing figh, Kate, ftop that falling tear;
Come, my pretty comrade, entertain no fear;
But, may Heav'n befriend us! Hark! the drums
 command:
Now I will attend you, Love, I kifs your hand.

Kate.*I can't ftop thefe tears, tho' crying I difdain;
But muft own 'tis trying hard the point to gain:
May good Heav'ns defend thee! Conqueft on
 thee wait!
One kifs more, and then I give thee up to fate.

* Both repeat this verfe, only Thomas fays, { Conqueft on me wait!
            { yield myfelf to fate.

SONG XLIII.

THE LASS OF PEATIE'S MILL.

The lafs of Peatie's mill fo bonny blyth

and gay, In fpite of all my fkill, hath

ftole my heart away. When tedding of the

hay, Bare-head-ed on the green, Love

midſt her locks did play, and wan - ton'd

in her een.

Her arms, white, round, and fmooth;
   Breafts rifing in their dawn;
To age it would give youth,
   To prefs them with his hand.
Through all my fpirits ran
   An extafy of blifs,
When I fuch fweetnefs fand,
   Wrapt in a balmy kifs.

Without the help of art,
   Like flow'rs which grace the wild,
Her fweets fhe did impart,
   Whene'er fhe fpoke or fmil'd;
Her looks, they were fo mild,
   Free from affected pride,
She me to love beguil'd;
   I wifh'd her for my bride.

O! had I all that wealth
   Hoptoun's high mountains fill,
Infur'd long life and health,
   And pleafure at my will;
I'd promife, and fulfil,
   That none but bonny fhe,
The lafs of Peatie's mill,
   Should fhare the fame with me.

I

SONG XLIV.

HAD NEPTUNE.

Had Neptune when firſt he took charge

of the ſea, been as wife, or at leaſt been as

merry as we, He'd have thought better on't,

and inſtead of the brine, Would have fill'd the

vaſt ocean with generous wine - - - - - - - -

- - - - - - - - - - - - - - - - - - would have

fill'd the vaſt ocean with generous wine.

What traffcking then would have been on the main,
For the fake of good liquor, as well as of gain,
No fear then of tempeft, or danger of finking,
The fifhes ne'er drown that are always a-drinking.

The hot thirfty fun would drive with more hafte,
Secure in the evening of fuch a repaft;
And when he'd got tipfey, would have taken his nap,
With double the pleafure in Thetis's lap.

By the force of his rays, and thus heated with wine,
Confider how glorioufly Phœbus would fhine,
What vaft exhalations he'd draw up on high,
To relieve the poor earth as it wanted fupply.

How happy us mortals, when bleft with fuch rain,
To fill all our veffels and fill 'em again;
Nay even the beggar that has ne'er a difh,
Might jump in the river and drink like a fifh.

What mirth and contentment, on every one's brow,
Hob as great as a prince, dancing after his plough,
The birds in the air as they play on the wing,
Altho' they but fip would eternally fing.

The ftars, who I think, don't to drinking incline,
Would frifk and rejoice at the fume of the wine;
And merrily twinkling would foon let us know,
That they were as happy as mortals below.

I 2

Had this been the cafe, what had we enjoy'd,
Our fpirits ftill rifing, our fancy ne'er cloy'd;
A pox then on Neptune, when 'twas in his pow'r,
To flip, like a fool, fuch a fortunate hour.

SONG XLV.

MY TEMPLES WITH CLUSTERS.

My temples with clufters of grapes I'll en-

twine, And barter all joys for a gob-let of wine,

And barter all joys for a goblet of wine. In

and forget her at Bacchus's tun; No longer I'll

run,--

But stop and forget her at Bac-chus's tun.

Yet why thus resolve to relinquish the fair ?
'Tis folly with spirits like mine to despair;
For what mighty charms can be found in a glass,
If not fill'd to the health of some favourite lass ?

'Tis woman whose charms every rapture impart,
And lend a new spring to the pulse of the heart;
The miser himself, so supreme is her sway,
Grows a convert to love, and resigns her the key.

At the sound of her voice sorrow lifts up her head,
And poverty listens, well pleas'd, from her shred ;
While age, in an ecstasy, hob'ling along,
Beats time, with his crutch, to the tune of her song.

Then bring me a goblet from Bacchus's hoard,
The largest and deepest that stands on his board ;
I'll fill up a brimmer, and drink to the fair ;
'Tis the thirst of a lover—and pledge me who dare !

I 3

SONG XLVI.

TWEED-SIDE.

What beauties does Flora difclofe, How fweet

are her fmiles u--pon Tweed, Yet Mary's ftill

fweeter than thofe, Both Nature and fancy

ex-ceed. No dai--fy nor fweet blufhing

rofe, Nor all the gay flow'rs of the field, Nor

Tweed gliding gent-ly thro' thofe, Such beau-

ty and pleafure does yield.

The warblers are heard in the grove,
　The linnet, the lark, and the thruſh,
The blackbird and ſweet cooing dove,
　With muſic enchant every buſh.
Come, let us go forth to the mead,
　Let us ſee how the primroſes ſpring;
We'll lodge in ſome village on Tweed,
　And love while the feather'd folks ſing.

How does my love paſs the lang day?
　Does Mary not tend a few ſheep?
Do they never carelefsly ſtray,
　While, happily ſhe lies aſleep?
Tweed's murmurs ſhould lull her to reſt:
　Kind nature indulging my bliſs,
To relieve the ſaft pains of my breaſt,
　I'd ſteal an ambroſial kiſs.

'Tis ſhe does the virgins excel,
　No beauty with her may compare;
Love's graces around her do dwell:
　She's faireſt where thouſands are fair.
Say, charmer, where do thy flocks ſtray,
　Oh! tell me at noon where they feed;
Shall I ſeek them on ſweet winding Tay,
　Or pleaſanter banks of the Tweed?

SONG XLVII.

THE MOMENT AURORA.

The moment Au - ro - ra peep'd in - to my

room, I put on my clothes and I call'd for my

groom : Will Whiſtle, by this, had uncoupl'd

the hounds ; Who lively and mettleſome friſk'd

o'er the grounds. And now we're all faddl'd,

fleet, dapple, and grey ; Who ſeem'd longing

to hear the glad ſound hark away ! Hark a-

way! Hark away! Who feem'd longing to

hear the glad found hark away!

'Twas now, by the clock, about five in the morn;
And we all gallop'd off to the found of the horn:
Jack Garter, Bill Babbler, and Dick at the goofe,
When, all of a fudden, out ftarts Mrs Pufs;
Men, horfes, and dogs, not a moment would ftay,
And echo was heard to cry, Hark, hark away!

The courfe was a fine one fhe took o'er the plain;
Which fhe doubl'd, and doubl'd, and doubl'd again;
Till at laft fhe to cover return'd out of breath,
Where I and Will Whiftle were in at the death:
Then, in triumph, for you I the hare did difplay;
And cry'd to the horns, my boys, Hark, hark away!

SONG XLVIII.

O GREEDY MIDAS.

O greedy Midas, I've been told, That what

you touch you turn to gold, That what you touch

you turn to gold.   O had I but a pow'r like

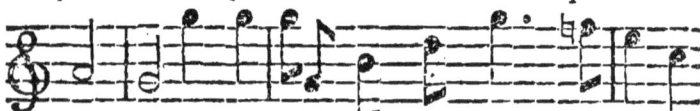

thine, O had I but a pow'r like thine, I'd tu - - -

- rn I'd

turn whate'er I touch to wine. I'd turn whate'er

I touch to wine.

Each purling ftream fhould feel my force,
Each fifh my fatal power mourn,
   Each fifh, &c.
And wond'ring at the mighty change,
   And wond'ring, &c.
Shou'd in their native regions burn,
   Shou'd in, &c.

Nor fhou'd there any dare t' approach
Unto my mantling fparkling fhrine,
   Unto my, &c.
But firft fhou'd pay their vows to me,
   But firft, &c.
And ftile me only god of wine.
   And ftile, &c.

SONG XLIX.

BUSH ABOON TRAQUAIR.

Hear me, ye nymphs, and ev' - - - ry fwain, I'll

tell how Peggy grieves me ; Tho' thus I languifh

and complain, Alas fhe ne'er believes me : My

vows and fighs, like fi - lent air, Un - heed - ed

ne - - ver move her, The bon - - ny bufh a-

boon Tra-quair, Was where I firft did love her.

That day fhe fmil'd and made me glad;
   No maid feem'd ever kinder:
I thought myfelf the luckieft lad
   So fweetly there to find her.
I try'd to footh my am'rous flame
   In words that I thought tender;
If more there pafs'd I'm not to blame;
   I meant not to offend her.

Yet now fhe fcornful flees the plain,
   The fields we then frequented;
If e'er we meet fhe fhows difdain,
   She looks as ne'er acquainted.
The bonny bufh bloom'd fair in May,
   Its fweets I'll ay remember;
But now her frowns make it decay;
   It fades as in December.

Ye rural pow'rs who hear my ftrains,
   Why thus fhould Peggy grieve me?
Oh, make her partner in my pains!
   And let her fmiles relieve me!
If not, my love will turn defpair;
   My paffion no more tender;
I'll leave the bufh aboon Traquair;
   To lonely wilds I'll wander.
        K

SONG L.

THE CUCKOW SONG.

When daisies pied, and violets blue, And la --

dy-smocks all sil - ver white, And cuckow-buds

of yellow hue, Do paint the meadows with de-

light; The cuckow then, on ev'ry tree, Mocks

marry'd men, Mocks marry'd men, Mocks marry'd

men; for thus sings he : Cuckow,   cuckow,

cuckow, cuckow, cuckow, cuckow; O word

of fear ! O word of fear ! Un-plea-fing to

a marry'd ear ; Unpleafing to a marry'd ear.

When fhepherds pipe on oaten ftraws,
    And merry larks are plowmen's clocks,
When turtles traed, and rooks and daws,
    And maidens bleach their fummer fmocks,
The cuckow then, on ev'ry tree,
Mocks marry'd men ; for thus fings he :
    Cuckow, cuckow ;---O word of fear !
    Unpleafing to a marry'd ear.

K. 3

SONG LI.

RULE, BRITANNIA.

When Britain, firſt, at Heav'n's command,

Aroſe - - - - - - - - from out the a - - zure main,

Aroſe from   out   the azure main, This was

the charter, the charter of the land, And guar-

dian an - - - gels ſung this ſtrain : Rule, Britan-

nia, Britannia, rule the waves, Britons ne - - -ver

ſhall be ſlaves.

The nations not fo bleft as thee
  Muft, in their turns, to tyrants fall ;
  Muft, in their turns, to tyrants fall ;
Whilft thou fhalt flourifh---fhalt flourifh great and
    free,
  The dread and envy of them all.
    Rule, Britannia, &c.

Still more majeftic fhalt thou rife,
  More dreadful, from each foreign ftroke ;
  More dreadful, from each foreign ftroke ;
As the loud blaft that---loud blaft that tears the fkies
  Serve but to root the native oak,
    Rule, Britannia, &c.

Thee haughty tyrants ne'er fhall tame ;
  All their attempts to bend thee down,
  All their attempts to bend thee down,
Will but aroufe thy---aroufe thy gen'rous flame,
  But work their wo and thy renown.
    Rule, Britannia, &c.

To thee belongs the rural reign ;
  Thy cities fhall with commerce fhine ;
  Thy cities fhall with commerce fhine ;
And thine fhall be the---fhall be the fubject main ;
  And ev'ry fhore it circles, thine,
    Rule, Britannia, &c.

The mufes, ftill with freedom found,
Shall to thy happy coafts repair :
Shall to thy happy coafts repair :
Bleft ifle ! with matchlefs—with matchlefs beauty
crown'd,
And manly hearts to guard the fair.
Rule, Britannia, &c.

SONG LII.

MA CHERE AMIE.

Ma chere amie, my charm - - - ing fair,

Whofe fmiles can banifh ev' - - ry care ; In kind

compaffion fmile on me, Whofe on - - - ly

care is love of thee. Ma chere a - - - mie;

Ma chere a --- mie ; Ma chere a - - mie ;

Ma chere a - - - - mie.

Under fweet friendfhip's facred name,
My bofom caught the tender flame.
May friendfhip in thy bofom be
Converted into love for me !
  · Ma chere amie, &c.

Together rear'd, together grown,
O let us now unite in'one !
Let pity foften thy decree !
I droop, dear maid ; I die for thee !
  Ma chere amie, &c.

SONG LIII.

THE WHISTLING PLOWMAN.

Recit.

The whiftling plowman hails the blufhing

dawn: The thrufh melodious drowns the ruftic

note: Loud fings the blackbird thro refound-

ing groves: And the lark foars to meet the ri-

fing fun.   Away to the copfe, to the copfe

lead away; And now my boys throw off the

hounds. I'll warrant he fhows us, he fhows us

fome play: See yonder he fkulks thro' the

grounds - - - - - - - - - See yonder he fkulks thro'

the grounds. Then fpur your brifk courfers,

and fmoke 'em my bloods ; 'Tis a delicate fcent

ly - ing morn ; What concert is equal to thofe

of the woods, Betwixt echo, the hounds, and

the horn ? The hounds and the horn, the hounds

and the horn, the hounds and the horn, ----

betwixt echo, the hounds and the horn.

Each earth, fee, he tries at in vain;
The cover no fafety can find;
So he breaks it, and fcowers amain,
And leaves us at diftance behind.
O'er rocks and o'er rivers and hedges we fly;
All hazards and dangers we fcorn.
Stout Reynard we'll follow until that he die:
Cheer up the good dogs with the horn.

And now he fcarce creeps thro' the dale;
All parch'd from his mouth hangs his tongue;
His fpeed can no longer prevail;
Nor his life can his cunning prolong.

From our ſtaunch and fleet pack 'twas in vain that
 he fled :
See his bruſh falls bemir'd forlorn !
The farmers with pleaſure behold him ly dead,
 And ſhout to the ſound of the horn.

SONG LIV.

AULD ROBIN GRAY.

When the fheep are in the fauld, And the ky

at hame, And a' the warld to fleep are gane,

The waes o' my heart fa' in fhow'rs frae my e'e,

When my gudeman lies found by me.

NEW SET OF AULD ROBIN GRAY.

Young Jamie lov'd me well, and afk'd me for

his bride, But fa - - ving a crown, he had nae-

thing elfe befide : To make the crown a pound

my Jamie gae'd to fea ; And the crown and the

pound were baith for me. He had nae been

gane but a year and a day, When my fa - ther

brak his arm and our cow was ftoun a - way ;

My mither fhe fell fick ; and Jamie at the fea ; and

auld Robin Gray came a - court - ing to me.

L

My father cou'dna work, my mother cou'dna fpin.;
I toil'd day and night, but their bread I cou'dna win :
Auld Rob maintain'd them baith, and, wi' tears in
    his e'e,
Said, " Jenny, for their fakes, O marry me !"
My heart it faid, Na ; and I look'd for Jamie back .
But the wind it blew hard, and the fhip it was a
    wrack ;
The fhip it was a wrack—why didna Jenny dee ?
O why was fhe fpar'd to cry, Wae's me ?

My father urg'd me fair ; my mither didna fpeak ;
But fhe looked in my face till my heart was like to
    break :
Sae I gae him my hand, but my heart was i' the fea,
And auld Robin Gray was gudeman to me.
I hadna been a wife a week but only four,
When, fitting fae mournfully ae night at the door,
I faw my Jamie's wraith, for I cou'dna think it he,
Till he faid, I'm come hame, love, to marry thee.

O fair did we greet, and little did we fay ;
We took but ae kifs, and we tore ourfelves away.
I wifh that I were dead ; but I'm no like to dee !
How lang fhall I live to cry, O wae's me !
I gang like a ghaift, and I downa think to fpin ;
I darena think on Jamie, for that wou'd be a fin.:
But I'll e'en do my beft a gude wife to be ;
For Auld Robin Gray is ay kind to me.

SONG LV.

THE DEATH OF AULD ROBIN GRAY.

Largo.

The summer was smiling, all nature round

look'd gay, When Jenny was attending on auld

Robin Gray : For he was sick at heart, and had

nae friend beside, But only me, poor Jenny, who

newly was his bride. Ah, Jenny, I shall dee,

he cry'd, as sure as I had birth ! Then see my

poor auld banes, pray, laid in the earth ; And

be a widow for my fake a twelvemonth and a

day, And I'll leave you whate'er belongs to

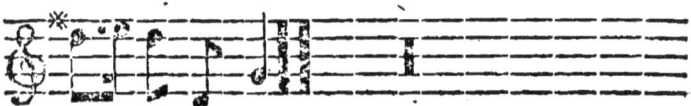

auld Robin Gray.

I laid poor Robin in the earth as decent as I could,
And fhed a tear upon his grave ; for he was very good.
I took my rock all in my hand, and in my cot I figh'd,
O wae's me ! what fhall I do fince poor auld Robin
    dy'd ?
Search ev'ry part throughout the land, there's nane
    like me forlorn,
I'm ready e'en to ban the day that ever I was born :
For Jamie, all I lov'd on earth, ah ! he is gone away,
My father's dead, my mother's dead, and eke auld
    Robin Gray.

I rofe up with the morning fun, and fpun till fetting
   day,
And one whole year of widowhood I mourn'd for
   Robin Gray;
I did the duty of a wife both kind and conftant too;
Let ev'ry one example take, and Jenny's plan purfue;
I thought that Jamie he was dead, to me or he was loft,
And all my fond and youthful love entirely was crofs'd;
I try'd to fing, I try'd to laugh, and pafs the time away,
For I had ne'er a friend alive fince dy'd auld Robin
   Gray.

* At length the merry bells rung round, I cou'dna
   guefs the caufe;
But Rodney was the man, they faid, who gain'd fo
   much applaufe.
I doubted if the tale was true, till Jamie came to me,
And fhow'd a purfe of golden ore, and faid it is for
   thee.
Auld Robin Gray, I find is dead, and ftill your heart
   is true;
Then take me, Jenny, to your arms, and I will be fo too:
Mefs John fhall join us at the kirk, and we'll be blithe
   and gay,
I blufhd, confented, and reply'd, adieu to Robin Gray.

* This verfe is to be fung quick.

SONG LVI.

DOWN THE BURN, DAVIE.

When trees did bud, and fields were green,

And broom bloom'd fair to fee, When Mary

was complete fifteen, And love laugh'd in

her e'e : Blyth Davie's blinks her heart did

move to fpeak her mind thus free ; Gang down

the burn, Davie, love, And I will fol-low thee.

Now Davie did each lad furpafs
That dwelt on this burn fide ;
And Mary was the bonnieſt lafs,
Juſt meet to be his bride.
Blyth Davie's blinks, &c.

Her cheeks were rofy, red and white,
 Her e'en were bonny blue,
Her looks were like Aurora bright,
 Her lips like dropping dew.
  Blyth Davie's blinks, &c.

What pafs'd, I guefs, was harmlefs play,
 And nothing, fure, unmeet;
For, ganging hame, I heard them fay,
 They lik'd a walk fo fweet.
  Blyth Davie's blinks, &c.

His cheeks to her's he fondly laid ;
 She cry'd, " Sweet love, be true ;
" And when a wife, as now a maid,
 " To death I'll follow you."
  Blyth Davie's blinks, &c.

As fate had dealt to him a routh,
 Straight to the kirk he led her,
There plighted her his faith and truth,
 And a bonny bride he made her.
No more afham'd to own her love,
 Or fpeak her mind thus free ;
" Gang down the burn, Davie, love,
 " And I will follow thee."

SONG LVII.

FRIEND AND PITCHER.

Moderato.

The wealthy fool with gold in ftore, Will ftill

defire to grow richer, Give me but thefe, I

afk no more, My charming girl, my friend and

Chorus.

pitcher. My friend fo rare, my girl fo fair,

with fuch what mortal can be richer? Give

me but thefe, a fig for care, With my

ſweet girl, my friend and pitcher.

From morning ſun I'd never grieve
    To toil a hedger or a ditcher,
If that when I come home at eve,
    I might enjoy my friend and pitcher.
        My friend ſo rare, &c.

Tho' fortune ever ſhuns my door,
    I know not what can bewitch her;
With all my heart can I be poor,
    With my ſweet girl, my friend, and pitcher.
        My friend ſo rare, &c.

SONG LVIII.

Tune---Friend and Pitcher.

THE filver moon that fhines fo bright,
  I fwear, with reafon, is my teacher ;
And if my minute-glafs runs right,
    We've time to drink another pitcher.
      'Tis not yet day, 'tis not yet day ;
        Then why fhould we forfake good liquor ?
      Until the fun-beams round us play,
        Let's jocund pulh about the pitcher.

They fay that I muft work all day,
  And fleep at night, to grow much richer ;
But what is all the world can fay,
    Compar'd to mirth, my friend, and pitcher.
      'Tis not yet day, &c,

Tho' one may boaft a handfome wife,
  Yet ftrange vagaries may bewitch her ;
Unvex'd I live a cheerful life,
    And boldly call for t'other pitcher ?
      'Tis not yet day, &c.

I dearly love a hearty man
  (No fneaking milk-fop Jemmy Twitchei),
Who loves a lafs and loves a glafs,
    And boldly calls for t'other pitcher.
      'Tis not yet day, &c.

SONG LIX.

MARY'S DREAM.

The moon had climb'd the high-eft hill,

Which ri - fes o'er the fource of Dee, And

from the eaftern fum - mit fhed Her fil - ver

light on tow'r and tree ; When Mary laid her

down to fleep, Her though ts on Sandy far

at fea, When foft and low a voice was

heard, fay, Ma-ry weep no more for me.

She from her pillow gently rais'd
   Her head, to afk who there might be.
She faw young Sandy fhiv'ring ftand,
   With vifage pale and hollow eye ;
" O Mary dear, cold is my clay,
  " It lies beneath a ftormy fea,
" Far, far from thee, I fleep in death,
  " So Mary, weep no more for me.

" Three ftormy nights and ftormy days
  " We tofs'd upon the raging main :
" And long we ftrove our bark to fave,
  " But all our ftriving was in vain:
" Ev'n then, when horror chil'd my blood,
  " My heart was fill'd with love for thee :
"   The ftorm is paft, and I at reft,
  " So Mary, weep no more for me.

" O maiden dear, thyfelf prepare,
  " We foon fhall meet upon that fhore,
" Where love is free from doubt and care,
  " And thou and I fhall part no more."
Loud crow'd the cock, the fhadow fled,
  No more of Sandy could fhe fee ;
But foft the paffing fpirit faid,
  " Sweet Mary, weep no more for me"

SONG LX.

HIGHLAND MARCH.

In the garb of old Gaul and the fire of

old Rome, From the heath-cover'd mountains

of Sco - tia we come: On thofe mountains

the Romans attempted to reign; But our

anceftors fought, and they fought not in

vain. Tho' no ci - - ty nor court of our gar*

M

ment approve, 'Twas prefented by Mars at

a fe-nate, to Jove; And, when Pallas ob-

ferv'd at a ball 'twould look odd, Mars receiv'd

from his Ve-nus a fmile and a nod.

No intemperate tables our finews unbrace;
Nor French faith nor French foppery our country dif-
    grace:
Still the hoarfe-founding pipe breathes the true martial
    ftrain,
And our hearts ftill the true Scottifh valour retain.
'Twas with anguifh and woe that, of late, we beheld
Rebel forces rufh down from the hills to the field;
For our hearts are devoted to George and the laws;
Aud we'll fight like true Britons, in liberty's caufe.

But ftill, at a diftance from Britain's lov'd fhore,
May her foes, in confufion, her mercy implore !
May her coafts ne'er with foreign invafions be fpread !
Nor detefted rebellion again raife its head !
May the fury of party and faction long ceafe !
May our councils be wife, and our commerce increafe ;
And, in Scotia's cold climate, my each of us find
That our friends ftill prove true, and our beauties,
  prove kind !.

SONG LXI.

To the foregoing Tune.

In the garb of old Gaul, wi' the fire of old Rome,
From the heath-cover'd mountains of Scotia we come
Where the Romans endeavour'd our country to gain ;
But our anceftors fought, and they fought not in vain.
  Such our love of liberty, our country, and our laws,
  That, like our anceftors of old, we ftand by freedom's
    caufe ;
  We'll bravely fight, like heroes bold, for honour and
    applaufe,
  And defy the French, with all their art, to alter our
    laws.

No effeminate cuftoms our finews unbrace ;
No luxurious tables enervate our race ;

Our loud-founding pipe bears the true martial ftrain ;
So do we the old Scottifh valour retain.
        Such our love, &c.

We're tall as the oak on the mount of the vale,
Are fwift as the roe which the hind doth affail :
As the full moon in autumn our fhields do appear,
Minerva would dread to encounter our fpear.
        Such our love, &c.

As a ftorm in the ocean when Boreas blows,
So are we enrag'd when we rufh on our foes ;
We fons of the mountains, tremendous as rocks,
Dafh the force of our foes with our thunderingftrokes.
        Such our love, &c.

Quebec and Cape Breton, the pride of old France
In their troops fondly boafted till we did advance :
But when our claymores they faw us produce,
Their courage did fail, and they fu'd for a truce.
        Such our love, &c.

In our realm may the fury of faction long ceafe !
May our councils be wife, and our commerce increafe,
And, in Scotia's cold climate, may each of us find
That our friends ftill prove true, and cur beauties
        prove kind ;
Then we'll defend our liberty, our country, and our
        laws,
And teach our late pofterity to fight in freedom's
        caufe ;
That they, like our anceftors bold, for honour and
        applaufe,
May defy the French and Spaniards to alter our laws.

SONG LXII.

POOR JACK.

Go patter to lubbers and fwabs, do ye fee,

'Bout danger and fear and the like, A tight

water boat and good fea-room give me, And

t'ent to a little I'll ftrike. Tho' the tempeft top-

gallant mafts fmack fmooth fhould fmite, And

fhiver each fplinter of wood, And fhiver each

M 3

fplinter of wood. Clear the wreck, ftow

the yards, and bouze ev'ry thing tight, And

under reef'd forefail we'll fcud :---Avaft, nor

don't think me a milk-fop fo foft, To be taken

for trifles a--back. For they fay there's a

providence fits up aloft, They fay there's a pro-

vidence fits up aloft, to keep watch for the life

of poor Jack.

Why I heard the good chaplin palaver one day;
  About fouls, heaven, mercy, and fuch,
And, my timbers, what lingo he'd coil and belay,,
  Why 'twas juft all as one as high Dutch ;
But he faid how a fparrow can't founder, d'ye fee,,
  Without orders that comes down below,,
And many fine things that prov'd clearly to me,.
That Providence takes us in tow;.
For fays he, do you mind me, let ftorms e'er fo oft
  Take the top fails of failors aback,
There's a fweet little cherub that fits up aloft.
  To keep watch for the life of Poor Jack.

I faid to our Poll, for you fee fhe would cry,,
  When laft we weighed anchor for fea,
What argufies fniv'ling and piping your eye ?
  Why what a damn'd fool you muft be :
Can't you fee the world's wide and there's room for
  us all,
  Both for feamen and lubbers afhore ; ;
And if to old Davy I fhould go friend Poll,'
  Why you never will hear of me more :

What then, all's a hazard, come don't be so soft,
Perhaps I may laughing come back,
For d'ye see there's a cherub sits smiling aloft,
To keep watch for the life of Poor Jack.

D'ye mind me, a sailor should be every inch
All as one as a piece of a ship,
And with her brave the world, without offering to
    flinch,
From the moment the anchor's a trip :
As for me, in all weathers, all times, sides, and ends,
Nought's a trouble from duty that springs,
For my heart is my Poll's, and my rhino my friend's,
And as for my life 'tis the king's.
Even when my time comes ne'er believe me so soft
As with grief to be taken abaok:
That same little cherub that sits up aloft,
Will look out a good birth for Poor Jack.

SONG LXIII.

THE BUD OF THE ROSE.

Her mouth, which a fmile, de--void of all

guile, half o - pens to view, is the bud of the

rofe, is the bud of the rofe, in the morning

that blows, impearl'd with the dew, impearl'd

with the dew; the bud of the rofe impearl'd

with the dew. More fragrant her breath.

than the flow'r fcented heath, than the flow'r

fcented heath at the dawning of day; the

hawthorn in bloom, the lily's perfume,

the lily's perfume or the bloffoms of

May. Her.

SONG XLIV.

THE GREENWICH PENSIONER.

'Twas in the good ship Rover, I fail'd the

world around, And for three years and o - ver

I ne'er touch'd Britifh ground, And for three

years and o—ver I ne'er touch'd Britifh ground;

At laft in England landed, I left the roaring

main; Found all relations ftranded, And went

to fea again : At laft in England landed, I left

the roaring main ; Found all relations ſtrand-

ed, And went to ſea again, And went to ſea

a - gain, And went to ſea a - gain ; Found all

relations ſtranded, And went to ſea again.

That time bound ſtraight to Portugal,
   Right fore and aft we bore ;
But, when we'd made Cap Ortugal,
   A gale blew off the ſhore :
She lay, ſo did it ſhock her,
   A log upon the main ;
Till, ſav'd from Davy's locker,
   We put to ſea again.

Next in a frigate ſailing,
   Upon a ſqually night,
Thunder and light'ning hailing
   The horrors of the fight.

My precious limb was loped off,
    I when they'd eas'd my pain,
Thank'd God I was not popped off,
    And went to fea again.

Yet ftill am I enabled
    To bring up in life's rear,
Although I'm quite difabled,
    And lie in Greenwich tier;
The king, God blefs his royalty,
    Who fav'd me from the main,
I'll praife with love and loyalty,
    But ne'er to fea again.

N

SONG LXV.

I TRAVERS'D JUDAH'S BARREN SAND.

I travers'd Judah's barren fand, At beauty's

altar to a-dore, But there the Turk had fpoil'd

the land, And Sion's daughters were no more.

In Greece the bold imperious mein, The wanton

look, the leering eye, Bade love's devotion not

L... c... cy is ne -ver nigh.

From thence to Italy's fair fhore
  I bent my never ceafing way,
And to Loretta's temple bore
  A mind devoted ftill to pray.
But there, too, Superflition's hand
  Had ficklied ev'ry feature o'er,
And made me foon regain the land,
  Where beauty fills the weftern fhore.

Where Hymen with celeftial pow'r
  Connubial tranfport doth adorn ;
Where pureft virtue fports the hour
  That ufhers in each happy morn.
Ye daughters of old Albion's ifle,
  Where'er I go, where'er I ftray ;
O charity's fweet children fmile
  To cheer a pilgrim on his way.

N 2

SONG LXVI.

PATTY CLOVER.

When little on the village green We play'd,

I learn'd to love her; She feem'd to me

fome Fairy Queen, So light tripp'd Patty Clo-

ver. Patty Clover, Patty Clover, Patty Clo-

ver, Patty Clover: So light,   fo light,   fo

light tripp'd Patty Clover.

With every fimple childifh art
    I try'd each day to move her ;
The cherry pluck'd the bleeding heart,
    To give to Patty Clover.
        Patty Clover, &c.

The faireft flow'rs to deck her breaft,
    I chofe—an infant lover ;
I ftole the goldfinch from its neft,
    To give to Patty Clover.
        Patty Clover, &c.

N 3

SONG LXVII.

IN MY PLEASANT NATIVE PLAINS,

In my pleafant na - tive plains, Wing'd

with blifs each moment flew; Nature there

infpir'd the ftrains, Simple as the joys I knew;

Jocund morn and evening gay, Claim'd the

merry, merry roundelay, Claim'd the merry

merry roun - de - lay.

Fields and flocks, and fragrant flow'rs,
    All that health and joy impart,
Call'd for artlefs mufic's pow'rs ;
    Faithful echoes to the heart.
Happy hours for ever gay, .
    Claim'd the merry roundelay.

But the breath of genial fpring,
    Wak'd the warblers of the grove ;
Who, fweet birds, that heard you fing :
    Wou'd not join the fong of love.
Your fweet notes and chantings gay,
    Claim'd the merry roundelay.

SONG LXVIII.

WHEN WILLIAM AT EVE.

When William at eve meets me down at

the ftile, How fweet is the nightingale's fong:

When William at eve meets me down at the

ftile, How fweet is the nightingale's fong:

Of the day I forget all the labour and toil,

Whilft the moon plays yon branches a - mong,

Whilſt the moon plays - - - - - - - - - - - - - -

- - - - - - - - - - - - - Whilſt the moon plays yon

branches among.

By her beams, without bluſhing, I hear him complain,
  And believe ev'ry word of his ſong :
You know not how ſweet 'tis to love the dear ſwain,
  Whilſt the moon plays yon branches among.

SONG LXIX.

HIGHLAND QUEEN.

No more my song shall be, ye swains,

Of purl - - ing streams, or flow'ry plains ; More

plea - sing beauties now in - spire, And Phœbus

tunes the warbling lyre ; Divinely aided, thus

I mean To ce - - le - - brate to ce - - le - brate

my Highland Queen.

In her, fweet innocence you'll find,
With freedom, truth, and beauty join'd;
From pride and affectation free,
Alike fhe fmiles on you and me;
The brighteft nymph that trips the green,
I do pronounce my Highland Queen.

No fordid wifh, or trifling joy,
Her fettled calm of mind deftroy;
Strict honour fills her fpotlefs foul,
And adds a luftre to the whole;
A matchlefs fhape a graceful mien,
All center in my Highland Queen.

How bleft that youth, whom gentle Fate
Has deftin'd for fo fair a mate;
Has all thefe wond'rous gifts in ftore,
And each returning day brings more:
No youth fo happy can be feen,
Poffeffing thee, my Highland Queen.

SONG LXX.

SHE ROSE AND LET ME IN.

The night her filent fa - ble wore, And

gloomy were the fkies ; Of glitt'ring ftars ap-

pear'd no more than thofe in Nel-ly's eyes.

When to her father's door I came, Where I

had of - ten been, I begg'd my fair, my love-

ly dame, to rife and let me in.

But she, with accents all divine,
　　Did my fond suit reprove ;
And while she chid my rash design,
　　She but inflam'd my love.
Her beauty oft had pleas'd before,
　　While her bright eyes did roll :
But virtue only had the pow'r
　　To charm my very soul.

Then who wou'd cruelly deceive,
　　Or from such beauty part ?
I loved her so, I could not leave
　　The charmer of my heart.
My eager fondnefs I obey'd,
　　Refolv'd she should be, mine,
Till Hymen to my arms convey'd
　　My treasure fo divine.

Now happy in my Nelly's love,
　　'Transporting is my joy :
No greater blessing can I prove,
　　So bless'd a man am I :
For beauty may a while retain
　　The conquer'd flutt'ring heart ;
But virtue only is the chain
　　Holds never to depart

SONG LXXI.

WHILE THE LADS OF THE VILLAGE.

While the lads of the village shall mer-ri-ly

ah, Sound their tabors, I'll hand thee a - long,

And I say unto thee, that ve - ri- ly ah, ve-

ri - ly ah, ve - ri - ly ah, ve - ri - ly ah, ve-

ri - ly ah, Thou and I will be first in the

.throng: - - - - - Thou and I will be first

in the throng.   Juſt then when the youth

who laſt year won the dow'r, With his mate

ſhall the ſports have begun ; When the gay

voice of gladneſs is heard from each bow'r,

D. C.

And thou long'ſt in thy heart to make one.

Thoſe joys that are harmleſs what mortal can

blame ? 'Tis my maxim that youth ſhould be

O 2

free ; And to prove that my words and my

deeds are the fame, to prove that my words

and my deeds are the fame, Believe thou fhalt

pre-fent-ly fee.   *Da Capo*,

SONG LXXII.

DEATH OF LUBAN.

Young Luban was a shepherd's boy, Fair Ro-

fa - lie a rustic maid; They look'd, they lov'd,

each other's joy, Together o'er the hills they

stray'd. Their parents saw and blest their love,

Nor would their happinefs delay; to-morrow's

dawn their blifs shall prove; To-morrow be

their wedding day.

When as at eve, beſide the brook,
   Where ſtray'd their flocks, they ſat and ſmil'd,
One lucklefs lamb the current took—
   'Twas Rofalie's—ſhe ſtarted wild.
" Run, Lubin, run—my fav'rite fave"—
   Too fatally the youth obey'd :
He ran, he plung'd into the wave
   To give the little wand'rer aid.

But ſcarce he guides him to the ſhore,
   When faint and funk, poor Lubin dies :
Ah Rofalie ! for evermore
   In his cold grave thy lover lies.
On that lone bank—oh ! ſtill be ſeen
   Faithful to grief, thou haplefs maid !
And with ſad wreaths of cyprefs green
   For ever foothe thy Lubin's grave.

SONG LXXIII.

THE TWINS OF LATONA.

The twins of La-to-na, fo kind to my boon,

Arife to partake of the chace ; And Sol lend

a ray to chafte Dian's fair moon, And a

fmile to the fmiles on her face. For the fport

I delight in the bright Queen of Love With

myrtles my brows fhall adorn, While Pan

breaks his chanter, and fkulks in the grove,

Excell'd by the found of the horn, by the

found of the horn - -- - - - - - - - - - - -

- - - - - - - - -- Excell'd by the found of the

horn. The dogs are uncoupled, and fweet is

their cry, Yet fweeter the notes of fweet e-

cho's reply. Sweet echo, fweet echo, Hark

forward, hark forward, the game is in view,

But love is the game that I wiſh to purſue,

But love is the game that I wiſh to purſue.

The ſtag from his chamber of woodbine peeps

out, His ſentence he hears in the gale, Yet

flies till entangled in fear and in doubt, His

courage and conſtancy fail. Surrounded by

foes, He prepares for the fray, Defpair tak-

ing place of his fear.   With antlers erected,

Slow.

a while ftands at bay, Then furrenders his life

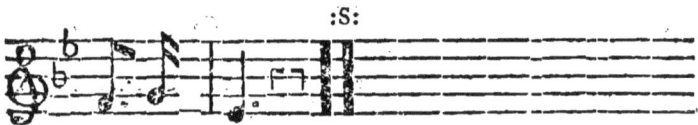

:S:

with a tear.   Da Capo al Segno.

SONG LXXIV.

EWE-BUGHTS MARION.

Will ye go to the ewe-bughts, Marion, And wear

in the fheep wi' me ? The fun fhines fweet, my

Marion, But nae half fae fweet as thee. The fun

fhines fweet, my Marion, but nae half fae

fweet as thee.

O Marion's a bonny lafs,
    And the blyth blink's in her e'e;
And fain wad I marry Marion,
    Gin Marion wad marry me.

There's goud in your garters, Marion,
  And filk on your white haufs-bane;
Fu' fain wad I kifs my Marion,
  At e'en when I come hame.

I've nine milk ewes, my Marion;
  A cow and a brawny quey,
I'll gi'e them a' to my Marion,
  Juft on her bridal day.

And ye's get a green fey apron,
  And waiftcoat of the London brown,
And vow but ye will be vap'ring,
  Whene'er ye gang to the town.

I'm young and ftout my Marion;
  Nane dances like me on the green;
And gin ye forfake me Marion;
  I'll e'en draw up wi' Jean.

Sae put on your pearlins, Marion,
  And kyrtle of the cramafie!
And foon as my chin has nae hair on,
  I fhall come weft, and fee ye.

SONG LXXV.

ERE BRIGHT ROSINA.

Ere bright Rofina met my eyes, How peace-

ful paft the joyous day; In rural fports I gain'd the

prize, Each virgin liften'd to my lay : But now no

more I touch the lyre, No more the ruftic fport

can pleafe, I live the flave of fond defire, Loft

to myfelf, to mirth and eafe.

The tree, which in a happier hour,
 Its boughs extended o'er the plain,
When blafted by the light'ning's pow'r,
 Nor charms the eye, nor fhades the fwain.
  The tree, &c.

P

SONG LXXVI.

AS DERMOT TOIL'D.

As Dermot toil'd one fummer's day, Young

Shelah, as fhe fat befide him, Fairly ftole his

pipe away, Oh, then, to hear fhe did deride

him. Where, poor Dermot, is it gone, Your

li - ly li - ly loo - - dle ? They've left you no-

thing but the drone, And that's yourfelf, you

noo - - dle. Beam, bum, boodle, loodle, loodle,

Beam bum, boodle, loodle, loo. Poor Dermot's

pipe is loſt and gone, And what will the poor

de-vil do?

Fait now I am undone, and more,
    Cried Dermot---Ah! will you be eaſy?
Did you not ſteal my heart before?
    Is it you have made a man run crazy?
I've nothing left me now to moan;
    My lily lily loodle
That uf'd to cheer me ſo, is gone,
    Ah! Dermot, thou'rt a noodle.

P 2

Beam, bum, boodle, loodle, loodle,
Beam, bum, boodle, loodle, loo,
My heart, and pipe, and peace, are gone,
What next will cruel Shelah do ?

Then Shelah, hearing Dermot vex,
　Cried, fait 'twas little Cupid mov'd me;
You fool, to fteal it out of tricks,
　Only to fee how much you lov'd me.
Come cheer thee, Dermot, never moan,
　But take your lily loodle ;
And, for the heart of you that's gone,
　You fhall have mine, you noodle.
　　Beam, bum, boodle, loodle, loodle,
　　Beam, bum, boodle, loodle, loo ;
Shelah's to church with Dermot gone ;
　And, for the reft---what's that to you?

SONG LXXVII.

LEWIS GORDON.

Very Slow.

O fend Lewis Gordon hame, And the lad I

winna name ; Tho' his back be at the wa', Here's

Chorus.

to him that's far awa.   Oh, hon, my High-

land man ! Oh, my bonny Highland man !

Weel would I my true love ken Amang ten

thoufand Highland men.

P 3

O to fee his tartan trews,
Bonnet blue, and laigh-heel'd fhoes.
Philibeg aboon his knee !
That's the lad that I'll gang wi'.

The princely youth that I do mean
Is fitted for to be a king :
On his breaft he wears a ftar :
You'd take him for the god of war.

Oh, to fee this princely one
Seated on his father's throne !
Difafters a' wou'd difappear :
Then begins the jub'lee here !

E.

SONG LXXVIII.

THE MAID THAT TENDS THE GOATS.

Up amang yon cliffy rocks, Sweetly rings the

rifing e-cho, To the maid that tends the goats,

Lilting o'er her native notes. Hark! fhe fings,

" Young Sandy's kind, An' he's promis'd ay to

lo'e me; Here's a brotch I ne'er fhall tin'd Till

he's fairly marry'd to me. Drive away, ye drone,

Time, An' bring about our bridal day.

" Sandy herds a flock o' fheep ;
" Aften does he blaw the whiftle,
" In a ftrain fae faftly fweet,
" Lammies, lift'ning, dare nae bleat.
" He's as fleet's the mountain roe,
" Hardy as the Highland heather,
" Wading thro' the winter fnow,
" Keeping ay his flock together,
" But a plaid, wi' bare houghs,
" He braves the bleakeft norlin blaft.

" Brawly he can dance and fing,
" Canty glee or Highland cronach ;
" Nane can ever match his fling
" At a reel, or round a ring.
" Wightly can he wield a rung ;
" In a brawl he's ay the bangfter ;
" A' his praife can ne'er be fung
" By the langeft winded fangfter,
" Sangs that fing o' Sandy
" Come fhort, tho' they were e'er fae lang."

SONG LXXIX.

THE STORM.

Ceafe, Rude Boreas, bluft'ring railer, Lift ye

landfmen all to me, Meffmates, hear a brother

failor fing the dangers of the fea, From bound-

ing billows firft in motion, When the diftant

whirlwinds rife, To the tempeft-troubled ocean,

where the feas contend with fkies.

Lively.

Hark ! the boatfwain hoarfely bawling,—
By topfail fheets, and haulyards ftand !
Down top-gallants quick be hauling !
Down your ftay-fails, hand, boys, hand !
Now it frefhens, fet the braces ;
   Quick the top-fail fheets let go ;
Luff, boys, luff, don't make wry faces !
Up your top-fails nimbly clew.

Slow.

Now all you on down-beds fporting,
   Fondly lock'd in beauty's arms,
Frefh enjoyments wanton courting,
   Free from all but love's alarms,—
Round us roar the tempeft louder ;
   Think what fear our mind enthralls.
Harder yet, it yet blows harder ;
   Now again the boatfwain calls.

Quick.

The top-fail yards point to the wind, boys,
   See all clear to reef each courfe !
Let the forefheets go ; don't mind, boys,
- Though the weather fhould be worfe.-
Fore and aft the fprit-fail yard get ;
   Reef the mizen ; fee all clear :
Hand up ! each preventer-brace fet ;
   Man the fore-yard ; cheer, lads, cheer !

Slow.

Now the dreadful thunder's roaring !
Peals on peals contending clafh !
On our heads fierce rain falls pouring !
In our eyes blue lightnings flafh !
One wide water all around us,
All above us one black fky !
Diff'rent deaths at once furround us,
Hark ! what means that dreadful cry ?

Quick.

The foremaft's gone, cries ev'ry tongue out,
O'er the lee, 'twelve feet 'bove deck.
A leak beneath the cheft-tree's fprung out;
Call all hands to clear the wreck.
Quick the lanyards cut to pieces !
Come, my hearts, be ftout and bold !
Plumb the well, the leak increafes,
Four feet water in the hold.

Slow.

While o'er the fhip wild waves are beating,
We for wives or children mourn ;
Alas ! from hence there's no retreating ;|
Alas ! from hence there's no return.
Still the leak is gaining on us,
Both chain-pumps are choak'd below,
Heav'n have mercy here upon us !
For only that can fave us now !

Quick.

O'er the lee-beam is the land, boys ;
 Let the guns o'erboard be thrown ;
To the pump come every hand, boys ;
 See our mizen-maft is gone,
The leak we've found, it cannot pour faft :
 We've lighten'd her a foot or more ;
Up, and rig a jury fore-maft ;
 She rights, fhe rights, boys ! wear off fhore.

Now once more on joys we're thinking,
 Since kind fortune fpar'd our lives ;
Come, the cann, boys, let's be drinking
 To our fweethearts and our wives.
Fill it up, about fhip wheel it ;
 Clofe to th' lips a brimmer join.
Where's the tempeft now ? who feels it ?
 None ! our danger's drown'd in wine !

SONG LXXX.

THRO' THE WOOD LADDIE.

O San - dy, why leaves thou thy Nelly to

mourn, Thy prefence could eafe me, when nai-

thing can pleafe me, Now dowie I figh on

the banks of the burn, Or thro' the wood lad-

die, un - til thou return. Tho' woods now

are gay, and mornings fo clear, while lavrocks

Q

are finging, and prim - ro - fes fpringing ; Yet

nane of them pleafes my eye nor mine ear,

When thro' the wood laddie ye dinna appear.

That I am forfaken, fome fpare na to tell:
   I'm fafh'd wi' their fcorning,
   Baith evening and morning ;
Their jeering gaes aft to my heart wi' a knell,
When thro' the wood, laddie, I wander myfell.

Then ftay, my dear Sandy, nae langer away,
   But, quick as an arrow,
   Hafte here to thy marrow ;
Wha's living in langour till that happy day,
When thro' the wood, laddie, we'll dance, fing and
   play.

SONG LXXXI.

HOW HAPPY THE SOLDIER.

How happy the foldier who lives on his pay,

And fpends half a crown out of fixpence a day;

Yet fears neither juftices, warrants, or bums,

But pays all his debts with the roll of his drums.

With row de dow, row de dow, row de dow,

dow; And he pays all his debts with the roll

Q 2

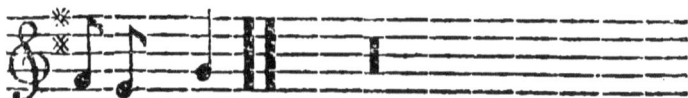

of his drums.

He cares not a marvedy how the world goes;
His king finds him quarters, and money, and clothes;
He laughs at all forrow whenever it comes,
And rattles away with the roll of his drums.
    With a row de dow, &c.

The drum is his glory, his joy and delight,
It leads him to pleafure as well as to fight;
No girl, when fhe hears it, tho' ever fo glum,
But packs up her tatters, and follows the drum.
    With a row de dow, &c.

SONG LXXXII.

BONNY BET.

No more I'll court the town-bred fair, Who

fhines in ar-ti-ficial beauty, For native charms,

without compare. Claim all my love, refpect,

and duty. Oh my bonny bonny Bet, fweet blof-

fom, Oh my bonny, bonny Bet, fweet bloffom,

Was I a king, fo proud to wear thee, From

off the verdant couch I'd bear thee, To grace

thy faith - ful lo - ver's bofom, O my bonny

bonny Bet.

Q3

Yet, afk me where thofe beauties lie,
I cannot fay in fmile or dimple,
In blooming cheek or radiant eye,
    'Tis happy nature wild and fimple.
    O my bonny, bonny Bet, &c.

Let dainty beaux for ladies pine,
And figh in numbers trite and common,
Ye gods one darling wifh be mine,
    And all I afk is lovely woman.
    O my bonny, bonny Bet, &c.

Come, deareft girl, the rofy bowl,
    Like thy bright eye with pleafure dancing,
My heaven art thou, fo take my foul,
    With raptnre every fenfe entrancing.
    O my bonny, bonny Bet, &c.

SONG LXXXIII.

OH NANNY WILT THOU FLY WITH ME?

Oh Nan-ny, wilt thou fly with me, Nor

figh to leave the charming town? Can fi-

lent glens have charms for thee, The low-ly

cote and ruffet gown? No longer dreft in filk-

en fheen, No longer deck'd with jewels

rare! Say, canft thou quit the bu-fy fcene,

Where thou wert faireſt of the fair ? Say,

canſt thou quit the bu - - fy fcene, Where thou

wert fair - - - eſt of - - - - the fair ?   Where

thou - - - wert faireſt, where thou - - - - wert

faireſt, where thou - - - - wert fair - eſt of the

fair ?

O Nanny when thou 'rt far awa,
　Wilt thou not caſt a wiſh behind ?
Say, can'ſt thou face the flaky ſnaw
　Nor ſhrink before the warping wind ?
O can that ſaft and gentleſt mien
　Severeſt hardſhips learn to bear ?
Nor, ſad regret each courtly ſcene,
　Where thou wert faireſt of the fair ?

O Nanny, can'ſt thou love ſo true,
　Thro' perils keen wi' me to gae,
Or when thy ſwain miſhap ſhall rue,
　To ſhare with him the pang of wae ?
And when invading pains befall,
　Wilt thou aſſume the nurſes care,
Nor, wiſhful, thoſe gay ſcenes recall,
　Where thou wert faireſt of the Fair ?

And when, at laſt, thy love ſhall die,
　Wilt thou receive his parting breath ?
Wilt thou repreſs each ſtruggling figh,
　And chear with ſmiles the bed of death ?
And wilt thou, o'er his much loved clay,
　Strew flowers, and drop the tender tear,
Nor then regret thoſe ſcenes ſo gay,
　Where thou wert faireſt of the Fair ?

SONG LXXXIV.

ALONE BY THE LIGHT OF THE MOON.

The day is departed, and round from the

cloud The moon in her beauty appears; The

voice of the nightingale warbles aloud The

mu-fic of love in our ears, Maria appear!

now the feafon fo fweet With the beat of the

heart is in tune; The time is fo tender for

lovers to meet Alone by the light of the

moon, alone by the light of the moon, alone

by the light of the moon, a-lone by the light

of the moon, a ---- lone by the light of

the moon.

I cannot when prefent unfold what I feel;
   I figh---Can a lover do more?
Her name to the fhepherds I never reveal,
   Yet I think of her all the day o'er.
Maria, my love! do you long for the grove,
   Do you figh for an interview foon;
Does e'er a kind thought run on me as you rove,
   Alone by the light of the Moon?

Your name from the ſhepherds, whenever I hear,
My boſom is all in a glow ;
Your voice, when it vibrates, ſo ſweet thro' mine ear,
My heart thrills---my eyes overflow.
Ye pow'rs of the ſky, will your bounty divine
Indulge a fond lover his boon ;
Shall heart ſpring to heart, and Maria be mine
Alone by the light of the Moon ?

SONG LXXXIV.

THE PLOUGH-BOY.

A flaxen-headed cow-boy, as ſim-ple as

may be, And next a merry plough-boy, I whiſt-

led o'er the lee ; But now a ſaucy footman, I

ſtrut in worſted lace ; And ſoon I'll be a butler'

And wag my jol-ly face : When Steward I'm

promoted, I'll fnip a tradefman's bill, My maf-

ter's coffers empty my pockets for to fill. When

lolling in my chariot, So great a man I'll be,

So great a man, fo great a man, fo great a

man I'll be, You'll forget the little plough-boy

that whiftled o'er the lee, You'll forget the

little plough-boy That whiftled o'er the lee.

R

I'll buy votes at elections,
　　But when I've made the pelf,
I'll ftand poll for the parliment,
　　And then vote in myfelf :
Whatever's good for me, fir,
　　I never will oppofe ;
When all my ayes are fold off,
　　Why, then I'll fell my noes.
I'll joke, harangue, and paragraph,
　　With fpeeches charm the ear,
And when I'm tir'd on my legs,
　　Then I'll fit down a peer.
In court or city honour,
　　So great a man I'll be,
You'll forget the little plough-boy
　　That whiftl'd o'er the lea.

SONG LXXXIV.

WHEN RURAL LADS AND LASSES GAY.

When ru-ral lads and laffes gay Proclaim'd the

birth of rofy May, When round the May-pole

on the green, The ruſtic dancers all were ſeen :

'Twas there young Jenny met my view, Her like

before I never knew : She ſung ſo ſweet and

danc'd ſo gay, A-las ſhe danc'd my heart a-

way : She ſung ſo ſweet, ſhe ſung ſo ſweet, ſhe

ſung ſo ſweet, and danc'd ſo gay, Alas ſhe

danc'd my heart away, Alas ſhe danc'd my

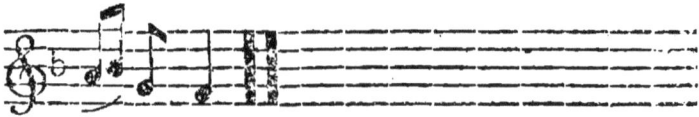

heart away.

At eve when cakes and ale went round,
I plac'd me next her on the ground :
With harmlefs mirth and pleafing jeft,
She fhone more bright than all the reft.
I talk'd of love and prefs'd her hand,
Ah ! who could fuch a nymph withftand !
Well pleas'd fhe heard what I could fay ;
Alas, fhe lur'd my heart away.
     She fung fo.fweet, &c.

She often heav'd a tender figh,
While rapture fparkled in her eye :
So winning was her face and air,
It might the coldeft heart infnare.
But when I afk'd her for my bride,
And (blufhing,) fhe to wed comply'd,
What youth on earth cou'd fay her nay,
Whofe charms might fteal all hearts away.
     She fung fo fweet, &c.

SONG LXXXVII.

AMYNTA.

My fheep I've for-fa-ken and left my fheep-

hook, And all the gay haunts of my youth I've

for - fook; No more for A - - myn - - ta frefh

garlands I wove : For ambition, I faid, would

foon cure me of love. Oh what had my youth

with am-bi-tion to do? Why left I A - myn-

ta? Why broke I my vow? O give me

my fheep, and my fheep-hook re-ftore, And I'll

wander from love and A - myn-ta no more.

Through regions remote in vain do I rove,
And bid the wide ocean fecure me of love;
O fool! to imagine that ought can fubdue
A love fo well founded, a paffion fo true.
    O what had my youth, &c.

Alas, 'tis too late at thy fate to repine!
Poor fhepherd! Amynta no, more can be thine;
Thy tears are all fruitlefs, thy wifhes are vain;
The moments neglected return not again.
    O what had my youth, &c.

SONG LXXVIII.

BEAUTY.

What is beauty, but a flow'r, A rofe that

bloffoms for an hour, Cherifh'd by the tears of

fpring, Fann'd by ev'ry zephyr's wing : See how

foon its colour flies, Blufhing, trembles, droops,

and dies. Age will come with wintry face, Ev'-

ry tranfient joy to chace ; Age will come with

win - - try face, Ev' - - ry tran - fient joy

:S:

to chace.

Friendfhip's but an empty name,
Glitt'ring like a vap'rifh flame ;
Youth flies faft and foon decays,
Blifs is loft while Time delays.
Deck, O, deck, your couch with flow'rs,
Laugh away the fportive hours ;
Then fince life's a fleeting day,
Ah ! enjoy it while you may.

SONG LXXXVIII.

THE WEDDING DAY.

What virgin or shepherd, in valley or grove,

Will en - vy my innocent lays, The song of the

heart, and the offspring of love, When sung in

my Corydon's praise. O'er brook and o'er brake

as he hies to the bow'r, How lightsome my shep-

herd can trip; And sure when of love he de-

scribes the soft pow'r, The honey-dew drops

from his lip : And sure when of love he de-

scribes the soft pow'r, The honey-dew drops

from his lip.

How sweet is the primrose, the violet how sweet,
  And sweet is the eglantine breeze,
But Corydon's kifs when by moonlight we meet,
  To me is far sweeter than thefe,
I blufh at his raptures, I hear all his vows,
  I figh when I offer to fpeak ;
And oh what delight my fond bofom o'er flows
  When I feel the foft touch of his cheek.

Refponfive and fhrill be the notes from the fpray,
  Let the pipe thro' the village refound ;

Be ſmiles in each face O ye ſhepherds to day,
  And ring the bells merrily round,
Your favours prepare my companions with ſpeed,
  Aſſiſt me my bluſhes to hide,
A twelvemonth ago on this day I agreed
  To be my lov'd Corydon's bride.

SONG LXXXIX.

GOLDEN DAYS OF GOOD QUEEN BESS.

To my mufe give attention, and deem it

not a myftery, If we jumble together mufic,

poetry, and hiftory : The times to difplay in

the days of Queen Befs. Sir, Whofe name and

whofe mem'ry po-fte-ri-ty may blefs, Sir. O the

golden days of good Queen Befs ; Merry be the

memory of good Queen Befs.

Then we laugh'd at the bugbears of dons and armadas,
With their gunpowder puffs, and their bluſtering
　　bravadoes;
For we knew how to manage both the muſket and
　　the bow, Sir,
And cou'd bring down a Spaniard juſt as eaſy as a
　　crow, Sir.
　　　　O the golden, days &c.

Then our ſtreets were unpav'd, and our houſes were
　　　thatch'd, Sir,
Our windows were lattic'd and our doors only latch'd,
　　Sir;
Yet ſo few were the folks that would plunder and
　　rob, Sir,
That the hangman was ſtarving for want of a
　　Job, Sir.
　　　　O the golden days, &c.

Then our ladies with large ruffs tied round about
　　the neck faſt,
Would gobble up a pound of beef ſteakes for their
　　breakfaſt;
While a cloſe quil'd-up coif their noddles juſt did fit,
　　　Sir,
And they truſs'd up as tight as a rabbit for the ſpit,
　　Sir.
　　　　O the golden days, &c.

S

Then jerkins, and doublets, and yellow woifted hofe,
    Sir,
With a huge pair of whifkers, was the drefs of our
    beaus, Sir;
Strong beer they preferr'd to claret or to hock Sir
And no poultry they priz'd like the wing of an ox'
    Sir.
      O the golden days, &c.

Good neighbourhood then was as plenty too as beef,
    Sir,
And the poor from the rich ne'er wanted relief, Sir;
While merry went the mill clack, the fhuttle and
    the plow, Sir,
And honeft men could live by the fweet of their
    brow, Sir,
      O the golden days, &c.

Then football, and wreftling, and pitching of the bar,
    Sir,
Were prefer'd to a flute, to a fiddle, or guitar, Sir:
And for jaunting, and junketting, the fav'rite regale,
    Sir,
Was a walk as far as Chelfea, to demolifh buns and ale,
    Sir.
      O the golden days, &c.

Then the folks, ev'ry Sunday, went twice, at leaft
 to church, Sir,
And never left the parfon or his fermon .in the
 lurch, Sir,
For they judg'd that the Sabbath was for people to be
 good in, Sir.
And they thought it Sabbath-breaking if they din'd
 without a pudding, Sir.
   O the golden days, &c.

Then our great men were good, and our good men
 were great, Sir,
And the props of the nation were the pillars of the
 ftate, Sir.;
For the fov'reign and fubject one intereft fup-
 ported,
And our powerful alliance by all powers then was
 courted
   O the golden days, &c.

Then the high and mighty ftates, to their everlafting
 ` ftain, Sir,
By Britons were releaf'd from the galling yoke of
 Spain, Sir,
And the rouf'd Britifh lion, had all Europe then
 combin'd, Sir,
Undifmay'd would have fcatter'd them, like chaff
 before the wind, Sir.
   O the golden days, &c.

Thus they ate, and they drank, and they work'd, and
   they play'd, Sir,
Of their friends not asham'd, nor of enemies afraid,
   Sir :
And little did they think, when this ground they ftood
   on, Sir,
To be drawn from the life, now they're all dead and
   gone, Sir.
     O the golden days, &c.

SONG XC.

THE GOLDEN DAYS WE NOW POSSESS ;

A Sequel to the favourite Song of Good Queen Befs.

To the foregoing Tune.

In the praife of Queen Befs lofty ftrains have been
   fung, Sir ;
And her fame has been echo'd by old and by young,
   Sir ;
But from times that are paft we'll for once turn our
   eyes, Sir,
As the times we enjoy 'tis but wifdom to prize, Sir,

Then whate'er were the days of Good
    Queen Befs,
Let us praife the golden days we now
    poffefs.

Without armies to combat, or armadas to withftand,
    Sir,
Our foes at our feet, and the fword in our hand, Sir,
Lafting peace we fecure while we're Lords of the
    feas, Sir,
And our ftout wooden walls are our fure guaran-
    tees, Sir,
        Such are the golden days we now poffefs,
        Whatever were the days of Good Queen
    Befs.

No Bigots rule the roaft, now, with perfecution dire,
    Sir,
Burning zeal now no more heaps the faggot on the
    fire, Sir :
No bifhop now can broil a poor Jew like a pigeon,
    Sir ;
Nor barbacue a Pagan, like a pig, for religion, Sir.
        Such are, &c.

Now no legendary faint robs the lab'rer of one day,
Except now and then when he celebrates St Monday :
And good folks, ev'ry fabbath, keep church without
    a pother, Sir,

By walking in at one door, and ftealing out at t'other,
  Sir.
      Such are, &c.

Then for drefs—modern belles bear the bell beyond
  compare, Sir,
Though farthingales and ruffs are got rather out of
  wear, Sir;
But when trufs'd up, like pullets, whether fat, lean,
  or plump, Sir,
'Tis no matter, fo they've got but a merrythought
  and rump, Sir,
      Such are, &c.

Such promontories, fure, may be ftyl'd inacceffibles,
As our fmall-cloaths, by prudes, are pronounc'd
  inexpreffibles ;
And the tafte of our beaus won't admit of difpute, Sir,
When they ride in their flippers, and walk about in
  boots, Sir.
      Such are, &c.

Our language is refin'd too, from what 'twas of yore,
  Sir,
As a fhoe ftring's the dandy, and a buckle's quite a
  bore, Sir ;
And if raif'd from the dead, it wou'd fure poze the
  noddle, Sir,
Of a Shakfpeare, to tell what's the Tippy, or the
  Twaddle, Sir.
      Such are, &c.

Then for props of the ſtate, what can equal in ſtory,
  Sir,
Thoſe two ſtately pillars, call'd a Whig and a Tory,
  Sir ;
Though by ſhifting their ground, they ſometimes get
  ſo wrong, Sir,
They forget to which ſide of the houſe they belong,
  Sir.

   Such are, &c.

But as props of their ſtrength and uprightneſs may
  boaſt, Sir,
While the proudeſt of pillars may be ſhook by a poſt
  Sir ;
May the firm friends of freedom her bleſſings inherit,
  Sir,
And her foes be advanc'd to the poſt which they
  merit, Sir.
  Then ſhall the golden days we now poſſeſs
  Far ſurpaſs the boaſted days of good Queen Beſs.

And as the name of Brunſwick claims duty, love,
  and awe, Sir,
Far beyond a Plantagenet, a Tudor, or Naſſau, Sir,
Let the ſceptre be ſway'd by the ſon or the ſire, Sir
May their race rule this land till the globe is on fire
  Sir ;
  And may their future days, in glory and ſucceſs,
  Far ſurpaſs the golden days we now poſſeſs.

SONG XCI.

WIVES AND SWEETHEARTS.

OR,

SATURDAY NIGHT.

'Tis faid we ven'trous die-hards, When we

leave the fhore, Our friends fhould mourn left

we return To blefs their fight no more. But this

is all   a notion Bold Jack can't underftand ;

Some die upon the ocean, And fome   on land.

Then fince 'tis clear, Howe'er we fteer, No

man's life's under his command; Let tempefts

howl, And billows rowl, And danger prefs,

Of thofe in fpight there are fome joys, Us jolly

tars to blefs; For Saturday night ftill comes,

my boys, To drink to Poll and Befs.

One feaman hands the fails, another heaves the log,
  The purfer fwops,
  Our pay for flops,
The landlord fells us grog.
  Thus each man to his ftation,
  To keep life's fhip in trim
What argufies noration,
  The reft is fortunes whim.

Cheerly my hearts
Then play your parts,
Boldly refolv'd to fink or fwim ;
The mighty furge
May ruin urge,
And danger prefs ;
Of thofe in fpight there are fome joys,
Us jolly tars to blefs.
For faturday night ftill comes, my boys,
To drink to Poll and Befs.

For all the world juft like the ropes aboard a fhip ;
Each man's rigg'd out
A veffel ftout,
To take for life a trip :
The fhrouds and ftays, and braces,
Are joys and hopes and fears ;
The halliards fheets and traces
Still as each paffion veers ;
And whim prevails
Direct the fails
As on the fea of life he fteers.
Then let the ftorm
Heaven's face deform,
And danger prefs ;
Of thofe in fpight there are fome joys
All jolly Tars to blefs.
For faturday night ftill comes, my boys,
To drink to Poll and Befs.

SONG XCII.

AN IRISH DRINKING SONG.

Of the ancients its fpeaking my foul you'd be

after, That they never got how come you fo,

Would you fe-ri-oufly make the good folks die

with laughter; To be fure their dogs tricks we

don't know: To be fure their dogs tricks we

don't know. With your fmalli-liow nonfenfe, and

all your queer bodderns, Since whifky's a li-

quor divine : To be fure the old ancients, as well

as the moderns, Did not love a fly fup of good

wine ; Did not love a fly fup of good wine.

Apicius and Æfop, as authors affure us,
　Would fwig 'till as drunk as a beaft,
Then what do you think of that rogue Epicurus,
　Was not he a tight hand at a feaft.
　　With your fmalliliow, &c.

Alexander the great at his banquets who drank
　hard,
　When he no more worlds could fubdue,
Shed tears, to be fure, but 'twas tears of the tank-
　ard,
　To refrefh him and pray would not you,
　　With your fmalliliow? &c.

Then that to'ther old fellow they call'd Ariftotle,
    Such a devil of a tipler was he,
That one night having taken too much of his bottle,
    The taef ftaggered into the fea.
      With your fmalliliow, &c.

Then they made what they called of their wine a
    libation,
    Which, as all authority quotes,
They threw on the ground——mufha, what bodera-
    tion,
    To be fure 'twas not thrown down their throats.
      With your fmalliliow, &c.

T

SONG XCIV.

THE LASS OF RICHMOND HILL.

On Richmond hill there lives a lafs, More

bright than May-day morn, Whofe charms all

other maids furpafs, A rofe without a thorn.

This lafs fo neat, with fmiles fo fweet, Has won

my right good will : I'd crowns refign, to call

thee mine, Sweet lafs of Richmond hill, fweet

lafs of Richmond hill, fweet lafs of Richmond

hill; I'd crowns refign to call thee mine, Sweet

lafs of Richmond hill.

Ye´zephyrs gay that fan the air,
  And wanton thro' the grove,
Oh whifper to my charming fair
  I die for her and love.
    This lafs fo neat, &c.

How happy will the fhepherd be,
  Who calls this nymph his own:
O may her choice be fix'd on me,
  Mine's fix'd on her alone.
    This lafs fo neat, &c.

SONG XCV.

I'D THINK ON THEE, MY LOVE.

In ſtorms when clouds obſcure the ſky, And

thunders roll, and lightning's fly, In midſt of all

theſe dire alarms, I think, my Sally, on thy

charms. The troubled main, The wind and rain, My

ar - dent paſ - - ſion prove ; Laſh'd to the helm,

Should ſeas o'erwhelm, I'd think on thee, my love,

I'd think on thee, my love, I'd think on thee,

my love; Lafh'd to the helm, fhou'd feas o'er-

whelm, I'd think on thee, my love.

When rocks appear on every fide,
And art is vain the fhip to guide,
In varied fhapes when death appears,
The thoughts of thee my bofom chcers,
  The troubled main,
  The wind and rain,
 My ardent paffion prove,
  Lafh'd to the helm,
  Shou'd feas o'erwhclm,
I'd think on thee my love.

But fhou'd the gracious pow'rs be kind,.
Difpel the gloom and ftill the wind,.

And waft me to thy arms once more,
Safe to my long-loft native fhore ;
    No more the main,
    I'd tempt again,
  But tender joys improve ;
    I then with thee,
    Shou'd happy be,
And think on nought but love.

SONG XCVI.

THE SOLDIER'S GRAVE.

Of all fenfations pi-ty brings, To proudly

fwell the ample heart, From which the will-

ing forrow fprings, In o --thers griefs that

bears a part : Of all fad fym-pa - thy's de-

light, The manly dig - ni - ty of grief ;

A joy in mourning that excites And gives

the an --xious mind re - - lief, And gives

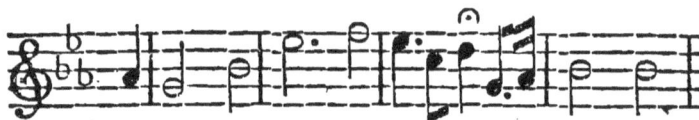

the anxious mind re - lief : Of thefe would

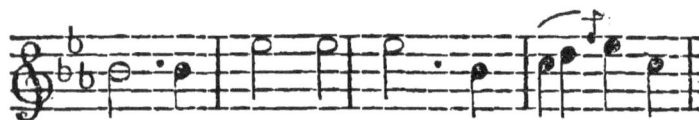

you the feel - ing know, Moft gen' - rous,

no - - ble, greatly brave, That ever taught

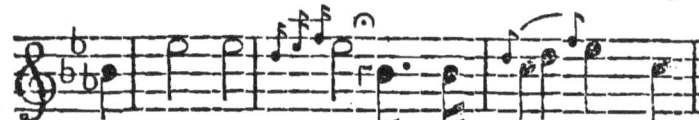

a heart to glow, 'Tis the tear that be -

dews a fol-dier's grave, The tear that be-

dews a fol - dier's grave.

For hard and painful is his lot,
Let dangers come, he braves them all ;
   Valiant perhaps to be forgot,
Or undiſtinguiſh'd doom'd to fall :
   Yet wrapp'd in conſcious worth ſecure,
The world that now forgets his toil,
   He views from a retreat obſcure,
And quits it with a willing ſmile.
   Then traveller one kind drop beſtow
'Twere graceful pity, nobly brave ;
   Nought ever bid the heart to glow
Like the tear that bedews a ſoldier's grave.

SONG XCVII.

DAVY JONES'S LOCKER.

OR,

A Sequel to the favourite Song of Poor Jack.

When laſt honeſt Jack, of whoſe fate I

now ſing, Weigh'd anchor and caſt out for

ſea ; For he never refus'd for his country and

king To fight, for no lubber was　he : To

hand, reef, and ſteer, and bouſe ev'ry thing

tight, Full well did he know ev'ry inch : Tho'

the toplifts of failors the tempeft fhould fmite,

Jack never was known for to flinch: Tho' the

toplifts of failors the tempeft fhould fmite, Jack

never was known for to flinch.

Aloft from the maft-head one day he efpied
Seven fail which appear'd to his view
Clear the decks, fpunge the guns, was inftantly cried,
And each to his ftation then flew;
'And fought until many a noble was flain,
And filenc'd was every gun;
Twas then that old Englifh valour was vain,
For by numbers, alas! they're undone.

Yet think not Bold Jack, tho' by conqueft difmay'd,
Could tamely fubmit to his fate :
When his country he found he no longer could ferve
Looking round, he addrefs'd thus each mate;
What's life, d'ye fee, when our liberty's gone,
Much nobler it were for to die,
So now for old Davy—then plung'd in the main;
E'en the Cherub above heav'd a figh.

SONG XCVIII.

NOTHING LIKE GROG.

A plague of thofe mufty old lubbers, Who

tell us to faft and to think, And patient fall in

with life's rubbers, With nothing but water to

drink : A can of good ftuff had they twigg'd

it, Would have fet them for pleafure a - - gog.

And fpite of the rules, And fpite of the rules

of the fchools, The old fools would have all

of 'em fwigg'd it, And fwore there was

nothing like grog.

My father, when laft I from Gninea
Return'd with abundance of wealth,
Cried---Jack, never be fuch a ninny
To drink---Says I---father, your health.

U

So I pafs'd round the ftuff—foon he twigg'd it,
And it fet the old codger agog,
And he fwigg'd, and mother,
And fifter and brother,
And I fwigg'd, and all of us fwigg'd it,
And fwore there was nothing like grog.

One day, when the Chaplain was preaching,
Behind him I curioufly flunk,
And, while he our duty was teaching,
As how we fhould never get drunk,
I tipt him the ftuff, and he twigg'd it,
Which foon fet his rev'rence agog.
And he fwigg'd, and Nick fwigg'd,
And Ben fwigg'd, and Dick fwigg'd,
And I fwigg'd, and all of us fwigg'd it,
And fwore there was nothing like grog.

Then truft me there's nothing as drinking
So pleafant on this fide the grave;
It keeps the unhappy from thinking,
And makes e'en more valiant the brave.
For me, from the moment I twigg'd it,
The good ftuff has fo fet me agog,
Sick or well, late or early,
Wind foully or fairly,
I've conftantly fwigg'd it,
And dam'me there's nothing like grog.

SONG XCVIII.

DONALD.

When first you courted me, I own, I

fond - ly fa - - - vour'd you, Ap - - pa - - rent

worth, and high re - - nown Made me be-

lieve you true, Do - nald. Each vir-tue

then feem'd to a - - - dorn The man e-

fteem'd by me, But now the mafk's

thrown off, I fcorn   to wafte one thought on

thee,   Donald.

O then for ever hafte away,
Away from love and me ;
Go feek a heart that's like your own,
And come no more to me, Donald.
For I'll referve myfelf alone,
For one that's more like me,
If fuch a one I cannot find,
I fly from love and thee, Donald.

SONG XCIX.

THE MELLOW TON'D HORN.

The grey-ey'd Aurora, in faffron ar-ray,

'Twixt my curtains in vain took a peep; And

tho' broader and broader ftill brightened the

day, Nought could roufe me, fo found did I

fleep: Nought could roufe me, fo found did I.

fleep. At length rofy Phœbus look'd full in

my face, Full and fervent, but nought would

not do ;　　Till the dogs yelped impatient

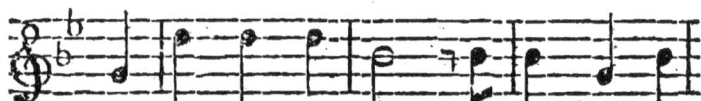

and long'd for the chace, And fhouting and

fhouting appear'd the whole crew, And fhout-

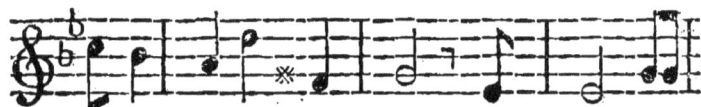

ing appear'd the whole crew. Come on, yoics

honies, hark forward, my boys, There ne'er was

fo charming a morn. Follow, follow, wake

Echo to fhare in our joys. Now the mufic, now

the mufic, now the mufic, now echo, now the

mufic, now echo, mark, mark, hark, hark, The

filver-mouth'd hound, and the mellow-toned horn.

Frefh as that fmiling morning from which they drew
 health,
My companions are ranged on the plain,
Bleft with rofy contentment that nature's beft wealth,
 Which Monarchs afpire to in vain,
Now fpirits like fire every bofom invade,
 And now we in order fet out,
While each neighbouring valley, rock, wood-land,
 and glade,
 Re—vollys the air rending fhout.

Come on yoics honies, hark forward my boys,
There ne'er was fo charming a morn :
Follow, follow, wake echo to fhare in our joys.
   Now the mufic—now echo—mark, mark,
   Hark, hark.
The filver-mouth'd hound and the mellow-toned
   horn.

Now Reynard's unearthed and runs fairly in view,
   Now we've loft him, fo fubtly he turns ;
But the fcent lies fo ftrong, ftill we fearlefs purfue,
   While each object impatiently burns,
Hark, babler gives tongue, and fleet, driver, and fly,
The Fox now the covert forfakes ;
Again he's in view, let us after him fly,
   Now now to the river he takes,
Come on, yoics honies, hark forward my boys,
There ne'er was fo charming a morn :
Follow, follow, wake echo to fhare in our joys.
   Now the mufic—now echo—mark, mark,
   - Hark, hark,
The filver-mouth'd hound and the mellow-toned
   horn.

From the river poor Reynard can make but one
   pufh,
No longer fo proudly he flies,
Tir'd, jaded, worn out, we are clofe to his brufh,
And conquer'd by numbers he dies :

And now in high glee to the board we repair,
Where fat, as we jovially quaff,
His portion of merit let every man fhare,
And promote the convivial laugh :
Come on, yoics honies, hark forward my boys,
We ne'er had fo charming a morn ;
As we followed, kind echo ftill fhared in our joys.
Now the mufic---now echo---mark, mark,
Hark, hark,
The filver mouth'd-hound and the mellow-toned
horn.

SONG C.

HOMEWARD BOUND.

Loofe ev'ry fail to the breeze, The courfe

of my veffel improve, I've done with the toils of

the feas, Ye failors! I'm bound to my love, Ye

failors! I'm bound to my love, Ye failors! I'm

bound to my love. I've done with the toils of the

feas, Ye failors! I'm bound to my love.

Since Emma is true as she's fair,
   My griefs I fling all to the wind,
'Tis a pleasing return for my care ;
   My mistress is constant and kind.

My sails are all fill'd to my dear :
   What tropick-bird swifter can move,
Who cruel shall hold his career,
   That returns to the nest of his love.

Hoist ev'ry sail to the breeze,
   Come, ship-mates, and join in the song ;
Let's drink while the ship cuts the seas,
   To the gale that may drive her along.

SONG CI.

GILDEROY.

Ah Chloris! cou'd I now but fit As un-

concern'd as when Your in - - - - fant beau-ty

cou'd beget No hap-pi-nefs nor pain.   When

I this dawning did admire, And prais'd the co-

ming day,   I lit - - - tle thought that ri - - fing

fire Wou'd take my reft a-way.

Your charms in harmlefs childhood lay
  As metals in a mine ;
Age from no face takes more away
  Than youth conceal'd in thine :
But as your charms infenfibly
  To their perfection prefs'd ;
So love as unperceiv'd did fly,
  And center'd in my breaft.

My paffion with your beauty grew,
  While Cupid, at my heart,
Still as his mother favour'd you,
  Threw a new fiaming dart.
Each gloried in their wanton part ;
  To make a lover, he
Employ'd the utmoft of his art ;
  To make a beauty, fhe.

X

SONG CII.

DATE OBOLUM BELISARIO.

O Fortune, how ſtrangely thy gifts are a-

warded, How much to thy ſhame thy caprice is

re-corded ; As the wife, great, and good, of thy

frowns feldom fcape a-ny, Witneſs brave Be-li-

fa-ri-us, Who begg'd for a halfpenny. Date o-

bolum, date obo-lum, date o-bolum Be-li-ſari-o.

He, whofe fame from his valour and vic'tries arofe,
Sir;
Of his country the fhield, and the fcourge of her foes,
Sir,
By his poor faithful Dog, blind and aged, was led,
Sir,
With one foot in the grave, thus to beg for his bread,
Sir.

Date obolum, &c.

When a young Roman knight, in the ftreet paffing
by, Sir,
The vet'ran furvey'd, with a heart-rending figh, Sir,
And a purfe in his helmet he dropp'd with a tear, Sir;
While the foldier's fad tale thus attracted his ear, Sir,
Date obolum, &c.

" I have fought, I have bled, I have conquer'd for
" Rome, Sir.
" I have crown'd her with laurels, which for ages
" will bloom, Sir;
" I've enrich'd her with wealth, fwell'd her pride
" and her power, Sir;
" I efpouf'd her for life, and difgrace is my dow'r, Sir.
Date obolum, &c.

" Yet blood I ne'er wantonly wafted at random,
" Lofing thoufands theirlives, with a nildefperandum;

" But each conqueſt I gain'd, I made friend and foe
　" know,
" That my foul's only aim was pro publico bono.

Date obolum, &c.

" I no colonies loſt by attempts to enſlave them ;
" I of Romans free rights never ſtrove to bereave
　" them ;
" Nor to bow down their necks to the yoke, for my
　" pleaſure,
" Have an Empire diſmember'd or ſquander'd its
　" treaſure.

Date obolum, &c.

" Nor yet for my friends, for my kindred, or ſelf, Sir,
" Has my glory been ſtain'd by the baſe views of pelf,
　" Sir,
" For ſuch ſordid deſigns I've ſo far been from carving
" Old and blind, I've no choice but of begging or
　" ſtarving.

Date obolum, &c.

" Now, if foldier, or ſtateſman, of what age or nation
" He hereafter may be, ſhou'd hear this relation ;
" And of eye-ſight bereft, ſhou'd, like me, grope his
　" way, Sir,
" The bright ſun-beams of virtue will turn night to
　" day, Sir,

Date obolum &c.

" So I to diftrefs and to darknefs inur'd, Sir,

" In this vile cruft of clay when no longer immur'd,
  " Sir,

" At death's welcome ftroke my bright courfe fhall
  " begin, Sir,

" And enjoy endlefs day from the funfhine within,
  Sir,

    Date Obolum, Date obolum, Date obolum Beli-
    fario.

SONG CIII.

THE CAN OF GROG.

When up the fhrouds the failor goes, And ven-

tures on the yard, The landman, he no better knows,

Believes his lot is hard, be-lieves his lot is

hard : Bold Jack with fmiles each danger meets,

Weighs anchor, heaves the log : Trims all the

fails, belays the fheets; And drinks his can of

grog : Bold Jack with ſmiles each danger meets,

Weighs anchor, heaves the log ; Trims all the

ſails, be-lays the ſheets, And drinks his can

of grog.

If to engage they give the word,
　To quarters he'll repair,
Now ſinking in the diſmal flood,
　Now quiv'ring in the air ;
Bold Jack with ſmiles each danger meets,
　Weighs anchor, heaves the log ;
Trims all the ſails, belays the ſheets,
　And drinks his can of grog.
　　　Bold Jack &c.

When waves 'gainſt rocks and quickſands roar,
   You ne'er hear him repine,
Tho' he's on Greenland's icy ſhore,
   Or burning in the line.
Bold Jack with ſmiles each danger meets,
   Weighs anchor, heaves the log ;
Trims all the ſails, belays the ſheets,
   And drinks his can of grog.
     Bold Jack, &c.

SONG CIV.

THE BANKS OF THE SHANNON.

In ſummer when the leaves were green,

And bloſſoms deck'd each tree, Young Teddy

then declar'd his love, His artleſs love to me :

On Shannon's flow'ry banks we fat, And there

he told his tale: " O Patty, fofteft of thy

fex, Oh let fond love prevail ; Ah, well-a-day

You fee me pine In forrow and defpair, Yet

heed me not, then let me die, And end my

grief and care."—" Ah no, dear youth, I foft-

ly faid, Such love demands my thanks ; And

here I vow eternal truth on Shannon's flow-

'ry banks.

And then we vow'd eternal truth,
On Shannon's flow'ry banks,
And then we gather'd fweeteft flowers,
And play'd, fuch artlefs pranks:
But woe is me the prefs-gang came,
And forc'd my Ned away,
Juft when we nam'd next morning fair,
To be our wedding day.

My love, he cry'd, they force me hence,
But ftill my heart is thine,
All peace be your's, my gentle Pat,
While war and toil is mine.
With riches I'll return to thee,
I fob'd out words of thanks,
And then we vow'd eternal truth,
On Shannon's flow'ry banks.

And then we vow'd eternal truth,
On Shannon's flow'ry banks,

And then I faw him fail away
And join the hoftile ranks.
From morn to eve, for twelve dull months,
His abfence fad I mourn'd,
The peace was made, the fhip came back,
But Teddy ne'er return'd.

His beauteous face and manly form,
Has won a nobler fair,
My Teddy's falfe, and I forlorn
Muft die in fad defpair.
Ye gentle maidens fee me laid,
While you ftand round in ranks,
And plant a willow o'er my head,
On Shannon's flow'ry banks.

SONG CVI.

THE SIEGE OF TROY.

I fing of a war fet on foot for a toy, And

of Paris and Helen and Hector and Troy, Where

on women, kings, gen'rals, and coblers you

ftumble, And of mortals and gods meet a very

ftrange jumble. Sing didderoo, bubberoo, Oh my

joy, how fwcetly they did cne another deftroy.

Come fill up your bumper, the whiſky enjoy,

May we ne'er ſee the like of the ſiege of Troy·

Menelaus was happy wid Helen his wife,
Except dat ſhe led him a devil of a life ;
Wid dat handſome taef Paris ſhe'd toy and ſhe'd play,
Till they pack'd up their awls and they both ran away,
    Sing didderoo, &c.

Agamemnon, and all the great chiefs of his houſe,
Soon took up the cauſe of this hornified ſpouſe ;
While Juno ſaid this thing and Venus ſaid that,
And the Gods fell a wrangling they knew not for what.
    Sing didderoo, &c.

Oh den ſuch a ſlaughter and cutting of trotes,
And ſlaying of bullocks and off'ring up goats ;
Till the cunning Ulyſſes the Trojans to croſs,
Clapt forty fine fellows in one wooden horſe.
    Sing didderoo, &c,

Z

Oh den for to fee the maids, widows and wives,
Crying fome for their virtue, and fome for their lives
Thus after ten years they'd defended their town,
Poor dear Troy in ten minutes was all burnt down.
    Sing didderoo, &c.

But to fee how it ended's the beft joke of all ;
Scarce had wrong'd Menelaus afcended the wall ;
But he blubb'ring faw Helen, and, oh ftrange to tell,
The man took his mare, and fo all was well,
    Sing didderoo, bubberoo, oh my joy,
How fweetly they did one another deftroy, :
Come ftill up your bumpers, the whifky enjoy,
May we ne'er fee the like of the fiege of Troy.

SONG CVII.

WHEN FIRST THIS HUMBLE ROOF I KNEW.

When firſt this humble roof I knew, With

various cares I ſtrove ; My grain was ſcarce, my

ſheep were few, My all of life was love.   By

mutual toil our board was drefs'd, The ſpring our

drink beſtow'd ; But when her lip the brim had

preſſ'd, The cup with nectar flow'd, with nec-

tar flow'd.

Content and peace the dwelling fhar'd,
   No other gueft came nigh ;
In them was given, tho' gold was fpar'd,
   What gold could never buy.
No value has a fplendid lot,
   But as the means to prove,
That from the caftle to the cot,
   The *all* of life is *love.*

SONG CVIII.

THE NEGLECTED TAR.

I sing the Britifh feaman's praife, A theme

renown'd in ftory; It well deferves more po-

lifh'd lays; O 'tis your boaft and glo-ry. When

mad-brain'd war fpreads death a-round, By them

you are protected ; But when in peace the na-

tion's found, Thefe bulwarks are neglected.

Then, Oh ! proteƈt the har-dy tar, Be mindful

of his me-rit, And when again you're plung'd in

war, He'll ſhew his daring ſpi--rit.

When thickeſt darkneſs covers all,
　Far on the trackleſs ocean.
When lightnings dart, when thunders roll,
　And all is wild commotion ;
When o'er the bark the white-top'd waves,
　With boiſt'rous ſweep are rolling,
Yet coolly ſtill, the whole he braves,
　Untam'd amidſt the howling. ．
　　Then, oh ! proteƈt, &c.

When deep immers'd in ſulphurous ſmoke.
　He feels a glowing pleaſure ;
He loads his gun—he cracks his joke,
　Elated beyond meaſure.

Tho' fore and aft the blood-ftain'd deck
   Should lifelefs trunks appear;
Or fhould the veffel float a wreck,
   The failor knows no fear.
      Then, oh! proteƈt, &c.

When long becalm'd on fouthern brime,
   Where fcorching beams affail him;
When all the canvas hangs fupine,
   And food and water fail him.
Then oft he dreams of Britain's fhore,
   Where plenty ftill is reigning;
They call the watch—his rapture's o'er,
   He fighs—but fcorns complaining.
      Then, Oh! proteƈt, &c.

Or burning on that noxious coaft,
   Where death fo oft befriends him;
Or pinch'd by hoary Greenland froft,
   True courage ftill attends him:
No clime can this eradicate;
   He glories in annoyance;
He fearlefs braves the ftorms of fate,
   And bids grim death defiance.
      Then, oh! proteƈt, &c.

Why fhould the man who knows no fear,
   In peace be then negleƈted?

Behold him move along the pier,
  Pale, meagre, and dejected.
Behold him begging for employ !
Behold him difregarded !
Then view the anguifh in his eye,,
  And fay, Are tars rewarded !
    Then, Oh ! protect, &c.

To them your deareft rights you owe ;
  In peace, then, would you ftarve them ?
What fay ye, Britain's fons ? Oh ! no !
Protect them and preferve them :
Shield them from poverty and pain,
  'Tis policy to do it.
Or when grim war fhall come again,,
  Oh, Britons, ye may rue it !
    Then, Oh ! protect, &c..

SONG CIX.

WHEN THE FANCY-STIRRING BOWL.

To the foregoing Tune.

WHEN the fancy ftirring bowl
　Wakes its world of pleafure,
Glowing vifions gild my foul,
　And life's an endlefs treafure ; .
Mem'ry decks my wafted heart,
　Frefh with gay defires,
Rays divine my fenfes dart,
　And kindling hope infpires.
　　　Then who'd be grave,
　　　When wine can fave
　　The heavieft foul from finking ;
　　　And magic grapes,
　　　Give angel fhapes
　　To ev'ry girl we're drinking.

Here fweet benignity and love
　Shed their influence round me,
Gather'd ills of life remove,
　And leave me as they found me.
Tho' my head may fwim, yet true
　Still to nature's feeling ;
Peace and beauty fwim there too,
　And rock me as I'm reeling.
　　　Then who'd be grave, &c.

On youth's foft pillow tender truth,
  Her penfive leffon taught me
Age foon mock'd the dream of youth,
  And wifdom wak'd and caught me.
A bargain then with love I knock'd,
  To hold the pleafing gipfey,
Then wife to keep my bofom lock'd,
  But turn the key when tipfey.
    Then who'd be grave, &c.

When time affuag'd my heated heart,
  The grey-beard blind and fimple,
Forgot to cool one little part
  Juft flufh'd by Lucy's dimple.
That part's enough of beauty's type,
  To warm an honeft fellow ;
And tho' it touch me not when ripe,
  It melts ftill while I'm mellow.
    Then who'd be grave, &c.

SONG CX.

THE MULBERRY TREE.

Behold this fair goblet, 'twas carv'd from

the tree, Which, Oh my fweet Shakefpeare, Was

planted by thee: As a relic I kifs it, and bow at

thy fhrine, What comes from thy hand muft be

e-ver divine, What comes from thy hand muft

be e-ver divine. All fhall yield to the mul-

berry tree, All ſhall yield to the mulberry tree·

Bend to thee, bleſt mulberry, Bend to thee, bleſt

mulberry. Matchleſs was he who planted thee,

And thou like him immortal ſhall be, And thou

like him immortal ſhall be.

Ye trees of the foreſt ſo rampant and high,
Who ſhoot out your branches, whoſe heads ſweep
   the ſky ;
Ye curious exotics, whom taſte has brought here,
To root out the nattves at prices ſo dear ;
   All ſhall yield to the mulberry tree·

The oak is held royal, is Britain's great boaft,
Preferv'd once our King, and will always our coaft;
Of the fiir we make fhips, there are thoufands that
    fight,
But one, only one, like our Shakefpear can write.
    All fhall yield to the Mulberry tree, &c.

Let Venus delight in her gay myrtle bow'rs,
Pomona in fruit trees and Flora in flowers;
The garden of Shakefpear all fancies will fuit;
With the fweeteft of flowers and the faireft of fruit.
    All fhall yield to the Mulberry tree, &c.

With learning and knowledge the well letter'd birch,
Supplies law and phyfic, and grace for the church;
But law and the gofpel in Shakefpear we find,
And he gives the beft phyfic for body and mind.
    All fhall yield to the Mulberry tree, &c.

The fame of the patron gives fame to the tree,
From him and his merits this takes its degree;
Give Phœbus and Bacchus their laurel and vine,
The tree of our Shakefpear is ftill more divine.
    All fhall yield to the Mulberry tree, &c.

As the genius of Shakefpear outfhines the bright day,
More rapture than wine to the heart can convey;

A a

So the tree which he planted by making his own,
Has the laurel and bays and the vine all in one.
　　All fhall yield to the Mulberry tree, &c.

Then each take a relic of this hallow'd tree,
From folly and fafhion a charm let it be ;
Fill to the planter the cup to the brim,
To honour your country, do honour to him.
　　All fhall yield to the Mulberry tree,
　　Bend to thee, blefs'd Mulberry :
　　Matchlefs was he who planted thee,
　　And thou like him immortal fhall be.

SONG CXI.

THE MILLER OF OXFORDSHIRE.

A miller I am, ever heart-whole and free,

A miller I am ever heart-whole and free, And

as juft, thank my ftars, as a miller fhould be :

fhou'd be, fhou'd be ; And as juft, thank

my ftars, as a mil-ler fhou'd be.

For while I dip my difh into each neighbour's

fack, For while I dip my difh in-to each neigh-

bour's fack, Like thofe better bred, I but live

by my clack, clack, clack,   clack, clack : Like

thofe better bred, I but live by my clack, clack,

clack, clack, clack, clack, clack, clack, clack.

Lawyers, doctors, and parfons, all follow my plan,
When their clack's fet a-going, they grind all they
 can ;
But my work's the cleaneft---for they grind in black,
While I grind in white, by the dint of my clack.

When fquire in the Parliament-houfe takes a poft,
Ding dong goes his clapper at fomebody's coft.:
If he gets into office, the cole he will fack,
Juft as I do my meal, by the help of my clack.

The gay folks of London may fneer if they will,
And fet their fine wits at a thief in a mill ;
But I'll do as I ought, if they'll fhew me the knack,
And let them, if they can, keep as honeft a clack.

A a 3

SONG CXII.

RUSSEL'S TRIUMPH.

Moderato.

Thurſday in the morn, the ninteenth of May,

Recorded for ever the famous Ninety two, Brave

Ruſſel did diſcern, by break of day, The lof-ty

ſails of France advancing to.·· All hands aloft they

cry, let Briti ſh valour ſhine, let fly a culverine,

the ſignal of the line, Let every man ſupply his

gun. Follow me, you fhall fee, That the battle

it will foon be won. Follow me, you fhall fee,

That the battle it will foon be won.

Tourville on the main triumphant rowl'd,
    To meet the gallant Ruffel in eombat on the
        deep ;
He led a noble train of heroes bold,
    To fink the Englifh admiral at his feet.
Now every valiant mind to vict'ry doth afpire,
The bloody fight's begun---the fea is all on fire ;
    And mighty Fate ftood looking on,
        Whilft a flood, all of blood,
    Fill'd the fcuppers of the Rifing Sun.

Sulphur, fmoke, and fire, difturbing the air,
    With thunder and wonder affright the Gallic
        fhore ;

Their regulated bands ſtood trembling near,
  To ſee their lofty ſtreamers now no more.
At ſix o'clock, the red, the ſmiling victors led,
  To give a ſecond blow, the fatal overthrow :
    Now death and horror equal reign :
    Now they cry, run and die,
    Britiſh colours ride the vanquiſh'd main.

See they fly, amaz'd, thro' rocks and ſands,
  One danger they graſp at, to ſhun the greater fate.
In vain they cry for aid to weeping lands,
  The nymphs and ſea-gods mourn their loſt e-
    ſtate.
For evermore, adieu, thou dazzling Riſing Sun,
From thy untimely end thy maſter's fate begun :
    Enough, thou mighty god of war :
    Now we ſing, bleſs the king !
    Let us drink to every Britiſh tar.

SONG CXIII.

ALL IN THE DOWNS.

All in the Downs the fleet was moor'd, The

ſtreamers waving to the wind, When black-ey'd

Suſan came on board, Oh where ſhall I my true

love find ? Tell me, ye jo-vial ſailors, tell me

true, Does my ſweet William, Does my ſweet

William ſail among your crew.

William, who high upon the yard
Rock'd with the billows to and fro,
Soon as her well-known voice he heard,
He figh'd, and caft his eyes below :

The cord glides fwiftly thro' his glowing hands,
And quick as light'ning on the deck he ftands.

So the fweet lark, high pois'd in air,
Shuts clofe his pinions to his breaft,
If chance his mate's fhrill call he hear,
And drops at once into her neft.

The nobleft captain in the Britifh fleet
Might envy William's lips thofe kiffes fweet.

O Sufan, Sufan, lovely dear,
My vows fhall ever true remain !
Let me kifs off that falling tear,
We only part to meet again.

Change as ye lift, ye winds, my heart fhall be
The faithful compafs that ftill points to thee.

Believe not what the landmen fay,
Who tempt with doubts thy conftant mind;
They'll tell thee, failors, when away,
In ev'ry port a miftrefs find.

Yes, yes, believe them, when they tell thee fo;
For thou art prefent wherefoe'er I go,

If to far India's coaft we fail,
    Thy eyes are feen in diamonds bright;
Thy breath is Afric's fpicy gale;
    Thy fkin is ivory fo white.
Thus every beauteous object that I view,
Wakes in my foul fome charm of lovely Sue.

    Though battle calls me from thy arms,
        Let not my pretty Sufan mourn ;
    Though cannons roar, yet, fafe from harms,
        William fhall to his dear return.
Love turns afide the balls that round me fly,
Left precious tears fhould drop from Sufan's eye.

    The boatfwain gave the dreadful word,
        The fails their fwelling bofom fpread ;
    No longer muft fhe ftay aboard :
        They kifs'd, fhe figh'd, he hung his head.
Her lefs'ning boat unwilling rows to land :
Adieu, fhe cries, and wav'd her lily hand.

SONG CXIV.

THE SAILOR'S SHEET ANCHOR.

Smiling grog is the failor's beſt hope, His

ſheet-anchor, his compaſs, his ca-ble, His log,

that gives him a heart which life's cares cannot

canker ; Though dangers around him unite to

confound him, Tho' dangers around him U--nite

to confound him, he braves them, And tips oʃf

his grog. 'Tis grog, only, grog is his rudder,

His compaſs, his cable, his log ; The ſailor's ſheet-

anchor is grog. What tho' he to a friend in truſt

his prize-money convey, Who, to his bond of

faith unjuſt, Cheats him and runs a--way. What's

to be done ? he vents a curſe 'Gainſt all falſe

hearts a -- ſhore. Of the remainder clears his

B

purfe, And then to fea for more, And then to

fea for more.   There, what tho' his girl, who

often fwore, To know no o-ther charms, He finds,

when he returns afhore, Clafp'd in a ri-val's

arms.   What's to be done ? he vents a curfe,

And feeks a kinder fhe :   Dances, gets groggy,

clears his purfe, Dances, gets groggy, clears his

purſe, and goes again to ſea. To croſſes born ſtill

truſting there, The waves leſs faithleſs than the

fair; There into toils to ruſh again, And ſtormy

perils brave. What then?——Smiling. *D. C.*

Bb 2

SONG CXV.

BESSY BELL AND MARY GRAY.

O Bef-fy Bell and Ma-ry Gray, they war'

twa bon-ny laf - fes, They bigg'd a bow'r on

yon burn brae, And theek'd it o'er wi' ra-

fhes. Fair Bef - fy Bell I lo'ed yeftreen,

And thought I ne'er cou'd alter, But Mary Gray,

twa pawky e'en, They gar my fan-cy fal-ter.

Now Beſſy's hair's like a lint-tap;
　She ſmiles like a May morning:
When Phæbus ſtarts frae Thetis' lap,
　The hills with rays adorning:
White is her neck, ſaft is her hand,
　Her waiſt and feet's fu' genty;
With ilka grace ſhe can command
　Her lips, O vow! they're dainty.

And Mary's locks are like a craw,
　Her een like diamonds glances;
She's ay fae clean, redd up, and braw,
　She kills whene'er ſhe dances:
Blyth as a kid, with wit at will,
　She blooming, tight, and tall is;
And guides her airs fae gracefu' ſtill—
　O Jove, ſhe's like thy Pallas!

Dear Beſſy Bell and Mary Gray,
　Ye unco fair opprefs us;
Our fancies jee between you tway,
　Ye are fic bonny laſſes:
Waes me! for baith I canna get,
　To ane by law we're ſtented;
Then I'll draw cuts and tak my fate,
　And be with ane contented.

SONG CXVI.

THE KISS.

One kind kifs before we part, Drop a

tear, and bid a --dieu. Tho' you fe-

ver, my fond heart, Till we meet, fhall pant

for you, Till we meet, Till we meet,

Till we meet, Shall pant for

you.

Yet, yet weep not fo my love,
   Let me kifs that falling tear,
Tho' my body muft remove,
   All my foul muft ftill be here.

All my foul and all my heart,
   Every wifh fhall pant for you,
One kind kifs, then, e'er we part,
   Drop a tear, and bid adieu.

SONG CXVII.

BRITANNIA,

OR,

THE DEATH OF WOLFE.

In a mouldering cave, a wretched retreat,

Britannia fat wafted with care : She wept for her

Wolfe, then exclaim'd againft Fate, And gave

herfelf up to defpair.   The walls of her cell fhe

had fculptur'd around With th' exploits of her

favourite fon; Nay, e-ven the duft, as it lay

on the ground, Was engrav'd with fome deeds

he had do - - - - - - - - - - - ne, Was engrav'd

with fome deeds he had done.

The fire of the Gods, from his chryftaline throne,
Beheld the difconfolate dame,
And, mov'd with her tears, fent Mercury down,
And thefe were the tidings that came :
" Britannia forbear, not a figh nor a tear,
For thy Wolfe fo defervedly lov'd ;
Thy grief fhall be chang'd into tumults of joy,
For Wolfe is not dead, but remov'd.

" The fons of the earth, the proud giants of old,
Have fled from their darkfome abodes ;
And, fuch is the news that in heaven is told,
They are marching to war with the Gods.
A council was held in the chamber of Jove,
And this was their final decree :

That Wolfe fhould be call'd to the army above,
And the charge was entrufted to me.

" To the plains of Quebec with the orders I flew ;
Wolfe begg'd for a moment's delay :
He cry'd, " Oh, forbear, let me victory hear,
" And then the commands I'll obey."
With a dark'ning film I encompafs'd his eyes,
And bore him away in an urn ;
Left the fondnefs he bore to his own native fhore
Might tempt again him to return."

SONG CXVIII.

HENRY AND MARIA,

OR,

THE SOLDIER's FAREWELL.

Henry.

The drums refound, the trumpet calls, The

parting moment is at hand ; The ftreamers on

Hibernia's walls To arms her freeborn fons com-

mand : Farewell, Ma-ri-a, ere I go; Farewel that

look, that ex - - - il'd woe, That nectar'd kifs, that

balmy blifs, And all that forms thee good as fair.

That nectar'd kifs, that balmy blifs, And all that

forms thee good as fair.

Maria.

And can you, Henry, part fo foon,
   Perhaps to view thefe bow'rs no more ?
Can love difplay no brighter boon
   Than perils on fome diftant fhore ?

Tho' fame prepares her trump for thee,
Ah ! think, my Henry, think on me :
To grief betray'd,
This form fhall fade,
And every virgin bloffom flee.

Henry.

O rend not thus this faithful breaft,
That lives, and warms, and throbs for thee :
If Conqueft perch on Valour's creft.
And Britain's glory rule the fea,
Yon crefcent moon's approaching wane
Shall view thefe longing arms again.
This frame entwine,
Nor more refign
The gem of Heaven's benign decree.

Maria.

Then go, thy King and country's pride,
Her ftrength and genius, as before,
When Gallia dreamt her fleets fhould ride
Triumphant to Irene's fhore :
Her native legions fought the field,
Her harp to ftring, her fair to fhield ;
With freeedom fir'd,
The world admir'd,
And vow'd each wreath that fame could yield.

SONG CXIX.

THE CELEBRATED DEATH-SONG

OF THE CHEROKEE INDIAN.

AN ORIGINAL INDIAN AIR.

The fun fets in night, and the ftars fhun

the day, But Glory re-mains when their lights

fade away: Begin, ye tormentors, your threats

are in vain, For the fon of Alk-no-mook fhall

never complain.

C c

Remember the arrows he fhot from his bow,
Remember your chiefs by his hatchet laid low :
Why fo flow ?—Do you wait till I fhrink from the
    pain ?
No !—the fon of Alknomook fhall never complain.

Remember the wood where in ambufh we lay,
And the fcalps which we bore from your nation
    away.
Now the flame rifes faft, they exult in my pain ;
But the fon of Alknomook can never complain,

I go to the land where my father is gone :
His ghoft fhall rejoice in the fame of his fon.
Death comes as a friend, he relieves me from pain :
And the fon of Alknomook has fcorn'd to com-
    plain !

SONG CXX.

THE BONNY BOLD SOLDIER.

I've plenty of lovers that fue me in vain, My

heart is with Wil-ly far o-ver the plain : For

handfome and witty and brave is the fwain ;

The bonny bold foldier young Willy's for me :

For handfome, and witty, and brave is the

fwain, The bonny bold foldier, young Willy's

C c 2

for me.   In the trumpet's fhrill found my

foldier delights ; For honour, his king, and his

country he figh - - - ts, he figh - - - - - - - - -

- -

- ts. Figh -

- - - - - - - - - - ts. For honour, his king,

and his country he fights. For honour, his

king, and his country he fights.

I fhare with his drefs, in the heart of a beau,
    The doctor my pulfe feels, and ne'er takes a fee
The one is pedantic, the other all fhow :
    The bonny bold foldier, young Willy, for me,
        In the trumpet's fhrill found, &c.

The lawyer fo crafty, I fly from in fear ;
    The dangling poet I fhun when I fee.
Once more, O ye powers, reftore me my dear,
    The bonny bold foldier, young Willy to me.
        In the trumpet's fhrill found, &c.

SONG CXXI.

YOUR MOUNTAIN SACK.

Your mountain-fack, your Fron-ti-ni-ac, To-

kay and twenty more, Sir ; Your Sherry and Per-

ry, That make men merry, Are De-i-ties I a-

dore, Sir: And well may Port our praife extort,

Where from his palace forth he comes, And glucks

and gurgles, fumes and foams. Gluck, gluck,

gluck, gluck, gluck, gluck, Gurgle, gurgle, gurgie,

gurgle, Gluck, gluck, gluck, gluck, Hickup,

hickup, hickup, gurgle and gluck, hickup, gurgle

and gluck.

The Briton, Sir John Barley-corn,
Stands highly in my favour;
His mantling head may well adorn
His valour and his flavour.
Nay, Cyder-an
Is a potent man,
When from his palace forth he comes,
And glucks and gurgles, fumes and foams,

Madeira monarch, him I fing!
And old Hock! lo another!

Champagne is my moft Chriftian king,
And Burgundy his brother,
Bold Bourdeaux, too,
Shall have his due,
When from his palace forth he comes !
And glucks and gurgles ! fumes and foams !

Old Rum, Arrack, and Coniac,
Are known for men of might, Sir ;
Nor fhall Sir Florence Flafket lack
A place among my Knights, Sir :
Don Calcavallo
Is a noble fellow,
When from his palace forth he comes !
And glucks and gurgles ! fumes and foams !

If fingly thus, each champion may
So many laurels gather,
Gods ! what a glorious congrefs they,
When all are met together !
When high in ftate,
Each potentate
Forth from his fpacious palace comes !
And glucks and gurgles ! fumes and foams !

SONG CXXII.

THE UPS AND DOWNS OF LIFE.

Of ups and downs we daily fee Examples

moft fur-pri-fing; The high and low of each

degree Now falling, are now rifing. Some up,

fome down, fome in, fome out, fome neither one

nor t'other; Knaves, fools, Jews, Gentiles, join

the rout, And joftle one another. With my

hey ho, Gee up, gee ho, hig-gle-dy, piggledy,

Truth, honour, honefty, trim, tram : For ho-

nefty's fcarce, honour's grown a mere farce,

And poor truth, baw, an ab-fo-lute whim

wham.

By ups and downs, fome folks, they fay,
 Among grandees have got, Sir,
Who were themfelves, but yefterday,
 The Lord knows who or what, Sir!
Sans fenfe or pence in merit's chair
 They doze and dream fupine, O!

But how the devil they came there,
 That neither you nor I know.
  With my heigho! &c.

Your country-maid comes up to town,
 A simple awkward body;
In half a year again goes down,
 No peacock half so gaudy.
"Lord, Ma'am," exclaims the lawyer's wife,
 With scandal ever ready,
" You see the ups and downs of life
 " Have made our Meg a lady."
  With my heigho! &c.

Virtue and Vanity lately are grown
 Mere buckets in a well, Sir;
The laſt gets up, the firſt gets down,
 As all the world can tell, Sir:
So many downs poor Virtue meets,
 Her ups so very few, Sir,
'Tis said she's naked met i' the ſtreets;
 But that is nothing new, Sir.
  With my heigho! &c.

Oh! what an age of ups and downs!
 " Hey, seven's the main," my Lord thrice
  knocks,
And lands and liberties, manors and towns,
 Are rattling in the dice-box.

Up fly the fools, on ruin bent,
  While they art full in feather ;
Get pluck'd, then rumbling down are fent,
  Whoop ! pell, mell, all together !
    With my heigho ! &c.

SONG CXXIII. .

O SAY, BONNY LASS.

O fay, bonny lafs, will you ly in a barrack ?

And marry a foldier, and carry his wallet ? O

fay would you leave baith your mither and dad-

dy, And follow the camp with your fol - dier

laddie ? O fay, would you leave baith your mi-

ther and daddy, And follow the camp with

your fol - - dier laddie ?

She.

O yes, bonny lad, I could ly in a barrack,
And marry a foldier, and carry his wallet;
I'd neither afk leave of my mither or daddy,
But follow my deareft, my foldier laddie.

He.

O fay, bonny lafs, would you go a campaigning?
And bear all the hardfhips of battle and famine ?
When wounded and bleeding, then wonldft thou
    draw near me ?
And kindly fupport me, and tenderly chear me ?

She.

O yes, bonny lad, I'll think naething of it,
But follow my Henry, and carry his his wallet:

D d

Nor danger, nor famine, nor wars can alarm me ;
My foldier is near me, and naething can harm me.

He.

But fay, bonny lafs, when I go into battle,
Where dying men groan, and the loud cannons
    rattle ?

She.

O then, bonny lad, I will fhare all thy harms,
And fhouldft thou be kill'd, I will die in thy arms

He.

O then, bonny lafs, I will fhare all thy harms,
And fhould I be kill'd, I will die in thy arms.

Both.

I ftill will be near thee, and fhield thee from harms.
And fhould I be kill'd, I will die in thy arms.

SONG CXXIV.

JEM OF ABERDEEN.

The tuneful lav'rocks chear the grove, And

sweetly smells the simmer green : Now o'er the

mead I love to rove Wi' bonny Jem of A-ber-

deen, bonny Jem of Aberdeen, bonny Jem of

Aberdeen : Now o'er the mead I love to rove

Wi' bonny Jem of Aberdeen. Whene'er we sit

D d.

beneath the broom, Or wander o'er the lee, He's

always wooing, wooing, wooing, always wooing

me. Whene'er we fit beneath the broom, Or

wander o'er the lee, He's always woo-

ing, woo-ing, woo-ing, al-ways woo-ing

me.

He's frefh and fair as flow'rs in May,
The blitheft lad of a' the green :
How fweet the time will pafs away
Wi' bonny Jem of Aberdeen.
Whene'er we fit, &c.

Wi' joy I leave my father's cot,
Wi' ilka fport of glen or green,
Weel pleaf'd to fhare the humble lot
Of bonny Jem of Aberdeen.
Whene'er we fit, &c.

Dd3

SONG CXXV.

BEN BACKSTAY.

Ben Backftay loved the gentle Anna, Con-

ftant as pu-r-ity was fhe ; Her honey-words,

like fucc'ring manna, Cheer'd him each voyage

he made to fea. One fatal morning faw them

parting, While each the other's forrow dried ;

They, by the tear that then was ftarting, They,

by the tear that then was ftarting, Vow'd they

be conftant till they died.

At diftance from his Anna's beauty,
   While roaring winds the fea deform,
Ben fings and well performs his duty,
   And braves for love the frightful ftorm.
Alas! in vain : the veffel, batter'd,
   On a rock fplitting, opened wide;
While lacerated, torn, and fhatter'd,
   Ben thought of Anna, figh'd, and died.

The femblance of each lovely feature,
   That Ben had worn around his neck,
Where art ftood fubftitute for nature,
   A tar, his friend, faved from the wreck :
In fervent hope while Anna burning,
   Blufhed as fhe wifhed to be a bride;
The portrait came, joy turn'd to mourning,
   She faw, grew pale, funk down and died.

SONG CXXVI.

ON THE GREEN SEDGY BANKS.

On the green fed-gy banks of the fweet:

winding Tay, As blithe as the woodlark that

carrols in May : On the green fedgy banks of

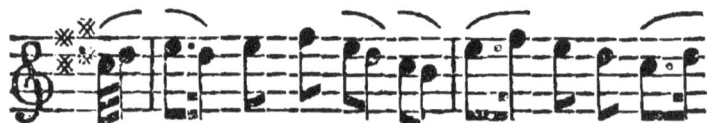

the fweet winding Tay, As blithe as the wood-

lark that carrols in May, 1 pafs'd the gay mo-

ments with joy and delight ; For peace cheer'd

each morn, And content crown'd the night:

Till love taught young hope my youth to de-

ceive : What we wifh to be true, what we wifh

to be true, what we wifh to be true, Love

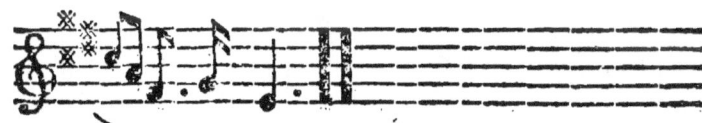

bids us believe.

Where-ever I wander, o'er hill, dale or grove,
Young Sandy wou'd follow with foft tales of love;
Enraptur'd he'd prefs me, then vow with a figh,
" If Jenny was cruel, alas ! he muft die."

A youth fo engaging with eafe might deceive,
What we wifh to be true, Love bids us believe.

He ftole my fond heart, then he left me to mourn,
For peace and content, that ne'er can return :
From the clown to the beau, the fex are all art,
They complain of the wound, but we feel the fmart ;
We join in the fraud, and ourfelves we deceive,
What we wifh to be true, Love bids us believe.

SONG CXXVII.

THE JOLLY FISHERMAN.

I am a jolly fifherman, I catch what I can

get,   Still going on my better's plan,   All's

fifh that comes to net :   Fifh, juft like men,

I've often caught, Crabs, gudgeons, poor John

Codfifh ; And many a time to market brought A

dev'lifh fight of odd-fifh, A dev'lifh fight of odd

fifh : Thus all are fifhermen through life, With

wary pains and labour : This baits with gold,

and that a wife, And all to catch his neighbour.

Then praife the jolly fifherman, Who takes what

he can get; Still going on his better's plan,

All's fiſh that comes to net, All's fiſh that comes

to net,   All's fiſh that comes to net. Still going

on his better's plan, All's fiſh that comes to net.

The pike to catch the little fry
  Extends his greedy jaw,
For all the world as you and I .
  Have ſeen your man of law :
He who to lazineſs devotes
  His time, is ſure a numb fiſh ;
And numbers, who give ſilent votes,
  May fairly be call'd dumb fiſh :
Falſe friends to eels we may compare,
  The roach reſembles true ones ;
Like gold-fiſh we find old-ones rare

Plenty as Herrings new ones.
Then praife the jolly Fifherman,
　　Who takes what he can get,
Still going on his better's plan,
　　All's fifh that comes to net.

Like fifh then mortals are a trade,
　　And trapp'd and fold and bought;
The old wife and the tender maid,
　　With tickling both are caught.
Indeed the fair are caught, 'tis faid,
　　If you but throw the line in,
With maggots, flies, or fomething red,
　　Or any thing that's fhining.
With fmall fifh you muft lie in wait
　　For thofe of high condition ;
But 'tis alone a golden bait
　　Can catch a learn'd Phyfician.
Then praife the jolly Fifherman,
　　Who takes what he can get,
Still going on his better's plan,
　　All's fifh that comes to net.

E e

SONG CXXVIII.

WHEN I WAS A YOUNKER.

When I was a younker, and liv'd with my

dad, The neighbours all thought me a fmart

little lad ; My mammy fhe call'd me a white-

headed boy, Becaufe with the girls I liked to toy.

There was Cifs, Prifs, Letty and Betty and Doll,

With Meg, Peg, Jenny and Winny and Moll :

I flatter their chatter fo fprightly and gay ;

I rumble 'em, tumble 'em ; that's my way.

One fine frofty morning a-going to fchool,
Young Moggy I met, and fhe call'd me a fool :
Her mouth was my primmer, a leffon I took ;
I fwore it was pretty, and kifs'd the book.
  But fchool,
    Fool,
      Primmer,
        and Trimmer,
          and Birch,
And boys for the girls I've left in the lurch,
  I flatter, &c.

'Tis very well known I can dance a good jig ;
And at cudgel s from Robin I won a fat pig :
I wreftle a fall, and a bar I can fling,
And, when o'er a flaggon, can fweetly fing.
  But Pig,
    Jig,
      Wicket,
        And Cricket,
          And Ball,
I'd give up to wreftle with Moggy of all.
  I flatter, &c.

SONG CXXIX.

BESS THE GAWKIE.

Blyth young Bels to Jean did fay, Will

ye gang to yon fun-ny brae, Where flocks do

feed, and herds do ftray, And fport a while wi'

Ja-mie? Ah, na, lafs, I'll no gang there,

Nor about Ja-mie tak' nae care, Nor about

Jamie tak' nae care, For he's ta'en up wi'

Mag-gie.

For hark, and I will tell you, lass,
Did I not fee young Jamie pafs,
Wi' mickle blithnefs in his face,
   Out o'er the muir to Maggy :
I wat he gae her mony a kifs,
And Maggie took them nane amifs ;
'Tween ilka fmack pleas'd her wi' this,
   " That Befs was but a gawkie."

" For whene'er a civil kifs I feek,
" She turns her head, and thraws her cheek,
" And for an hour fhe'll hardly fpeak ;
   " Who'd not ca' her a gawkie ?
" But fure my Maggie has mair fenfe,
" She'll gie a fcore without offence ;
" Now gie me ane unto the menfe,
   " And ye fhall be my dawtie."

" O Jamie ye hae mony tane,
" But I will ne'er ftand up for ane,
" Or twa, when we do meet again,
   " So ne'er think me a gawkie."
" Ah na, lafs, that cannot be ;

E e 3

" Sic thoughts as thefe are far frae me,
" Or ony thy fweet face that fee,
  " E'er to think thee a gawkie."

But, whifht, nae mair of this we'll fpeak,
For yonder Jamie does us meet;
Inftead of Meg he kifs'd fae fweet,
  I trow he likes the gawkie.
       Jamie.
" O dear Befs, I hardly knew,
" When I came by, your gown fae new;
" I think you've got it wet wi' dew"—
Quoth fhe, " That's like a gawkie :

" It's wat wi' dew, and 'twill get rain,
" And I'll get gowns when it is gane ;
" Sae ye may gang the gate ye came,
  " And tell it to your dawtie "
The guilt appear'd in Jamie's cheek ;
He cry'd, " O cruel maid, but fweet,
" If I fhould gang anither gate,
  " I ne'er cou'd meet my dawtie."

The laffes faft frae him they flew,
And left poor Jamie fair to rue,
That ever Maggie's face he knew,
  Or yet ca'd Befs a gawkie.
As they gaed o'er the muir they fang,
The hills and dales with echo rang,
The hills and dales with echo rang,
  " Gang o'er the muir to Maggy."

SONG CXXX.

YE SLUGGARDS.

Ye fluggards, who murder your lifetime in

fleep, Awake and purfue the fleet hare. From

life, fay, what joy, fay, what pleafure you reap,

That e'er cou'd with hunting compare? That e'er

cou'd with hunt - - - - - - - - - - - - - - - -

- - - - - - - - - - - - - - - ing compare.

That e'er cou'd with hunting compare, That

e'er cou'd with hunting compare. When Phœ-

bus begins to enlighten the morn, The huntfman,

attended by hounds, Rejoices and glows at the

found of the horn, Whilft woods the fweet echo

refound, Whilft woods the fweet e - - - - - -

- - - - - - cho refound, While woods the fweet

echo refound, While woods the fweet echo

refound.

The courtier, the lawyer, the prieft have a view,
   Nay ev'ry profeffion the fame,
But fportfmen, ye mortals, no pleafures purfue,
   But fuch as accrue from the game.
While drunkards are pleas'd in the joys of the cup,
   And turn into day ev'ry night,
At the break of each morn the huntfman is up,
   And bounds o'er the lawns with delight.

Then quickly, my lads, to the foreft repair,
   O'er hills, dales, and vallies let's fly,
For who can, ye gods, feel a moment of care,
   When each joy will another fupply?
Thus each morning, each day, in raptures, we pafs,
   And defire no comfort to fhare,
But at night to refrefh with the bottle and glafs,
   And feed on the fpoil of the hare.

SONG CXXXI.

NANCY OF THE DALE.

My Nancy leaves the ru - ral train, A camp's

diftrefs to prove,   All other ills fhe can fuftain,

But liv - - - - - - ing from her love : Yet, dear-

eft, tho' your foldier's there, Will not your fpi-

rit fail, To mark the hardfhips you muft fhare,

Dear Nan - cy of the dale, Dear Nan - cy

Dear Nan-cy, Dear Nan - - cy of the dale.

Or ſhould you, love, each danger ſcorn,
  Ah ! how ſhall I ſecure
Your health, 'mid toils which you were born
  To ſoothe—but not endure.
A thouſand perils I muſt view,
  A thouſand ills aſſail ;
Nor muſt I tremble e'en for you,
  Dear Nancy of the dale.

SONG CXXXII.

FIDELE'S TOMB.

To fair Fide-le's glaf-fy tomb, Soft maids

and village hinds fhall bring Each op'ning fweet

of earlieft bloom, And rifle all the breath - ing

fpring.

No wailing ghoft fhall dare appear,
  To vex with fhrieks this quiet grove ;
But fhepherd lads affemble here,
  And tender virgins own their love.

No wither'd witch fhall here be feen.
  No goblins lead their nightly crew ;
But female fays fhall haunt the green,
  And deck thy grave with pearly dew.

The red-breaft oft at evening hours
   Shall kindly lend its little aid,
With hoary mofs and gather'd flow'rs,
   To deck the ground where thou art laid,

When howling winds and beating rain,
   In tempeft fhake the Sylvan cell ;
Or midft the chace upon the plain,
   The tender thought on thee fhall dwell.

Each lonely fcene fhall thee reftore,
   For thee the tear be daily fhed :
Belov'd till life could charm no more,
   And mourn'd till Pity's felf is dead.

F f

SONG CXXXIII.

WHAT PLEASURE TO THINK.

What pleafure to think on the times we

have feen, 'Twas May-day I firſt faw my

Tom on the green, So neat was I drefs'd,

and fo fprightly a mien, A King was my lo-

ver, and I was his Queen. The garland pre-

fented by Tommy, How fweet from the hands

of my Tommy, The garland prefented by

Tommy, How fweet from the hands of my

Tommy.

A fide-look I threw on my lover by chance,
Which ftraight he return'd with as tender a glance,
My heart leap'd with joy when I faw him advance,
And weel did I guefs 'twas to lead up the dance ;
     For none danc'd fo neat as my Tommy,
     In all things compleat was my Tommy.

Beneath a gay woodwine with myrtles entwin'd,
And cowflips and violets, one ev'ning reclin'd ;
So charming a place, and the feafon fo kind,
He artfully chofe to difcover his mind :
     So fweet were the vows of my Tommy,
     And I could not refufe my dear Tommy.

SONG CXXXIV.

OLD ENGLAND'S WOODEN WALLS.

Thro' waves and wind, in days that are no

more, I held the helm, and ne'er ran foul of

fhore ; In pitch dark night my reck'ning prov'd

fo true, In pitch dark night my reck'ning

prov'd fo true, I rode out fafe the hardeft

gale that blew, I rode out fafe the hardeft

gale that blew: And when for fight the fig-

nal high was fhewn, Thro' fmoke and fire

Bob Boreas ftraight bore down: But tho' my

timbers are not fit for fea, Old England's

wooden walls my toaft fhall be. Old England's

wooden walls, Old England's wooden walls, Old

England's wooden walls my toaft fhall be. Old

F f 3

England's wooden walls, Old England's wood-

en walls, Old England's wooden walls my

toaſt ſhall be.

From age to age, as ancient ſtory ſhews,
We rul'd the deep, in ſpite of envious foes ;
And ſtill aloft, tho' worlds combine, we'll riſe,
Now all at home are ſplic'd in friendly ties :
In loud broadſides we'll tell both France and Spain,
We're own'd by Neptune ſov'reigns of the main.
O ! wou'd my timbers now were fit for ſea !
Yet England's wooden walls my toaſt ſhall be.

SONG CXXV.

LOVELY GODDESS.

Lovely goddefs, fprightly May, Faireft daughter

of the day, Hither come, with rofes crown'd,

Painting, as you tread the ground, Painting, as

you tread the ground. Tulips rear their glit'ring

heads, Pinks beftrow their fragrant beds, Wood-

bines fpangled o'er with dew, Deck their arbo-

rets for you, Deck their ar - bo - rets for you.

Hear the birds around thee fing
In the gardens of the fpring ;
Ev'y bufh and ev'ry tree
Warbles forth its joy to thee.
Nature's fongfters all are gay
At the lov'd approach of May ;
All, great Queen, thy praifes fing,
Thine, great Emprefs of the fpring.

Goddefs, in thy veft of green ;
Goddefs, with thy youthful mien ;
Hafte, and bring thy mines of wealth,
Gladnefs, and her parent, health ;
Bring with thee thy chearful train,
Chacing care, and chacing pain,
See, the lovely Graces, all
Throng obedient at thy call.

Goddefs, hafte, and bring with thee
Virtue's child, fair Liberty;
For, if Liberty's away,
Who can tafte the month of May ?
Here he comes, I hear the found
Of the merry fongfters round :

Here he comes, all frefh and gay,
Paying homage to thee, May.

Goddefs, who perfum'ft the air,
Who haft deck'd the earth fo fair ;
Thou, with gladnefs by thy fide,
Still'ft the raging of the tide ;
Bidft the winds forbear to roar,
And ftern winter feen no more ;
Meads and groves their echos ring,
Love himfelf is on the wing.

Lovely nymph, divineft May,
Thou to whom this verfe I pay ;
O ! thy healing warmth impart
To the miftrefs of my heart.
Ev'ry day with gladnefs crown,
By her health, preferve my own :
Blooming nymph, of heavenly birth,
Goddefs, thou, of health and mirth.

SONG CXXXVI.

TULLOCHGORUM.

Fidlers, your pins in temper fix,
And rofet weel your fiddle-fticks;
But banifh vile Italian tricks
    Frae out your quorum :]
Nor *fortes* wi' *pianos* mix,
    Gie's *Tullochgorum.*.   FERGUSSON.

Come gie's a fong, the lady cried, And lay your

difputes all afide; What nonfenfe is't for folks to

chide For what's been done before them. Let whig

and tory all agree, Whig and tory, Whig and tory,

Whig and tory all agree To drop their whig-meg-

morum. Let whig and tory all agree To spend the

night wi' mirth and glee, And cheerfu' sing alang

wi' me The reel of Tullochgorum.

Tullochgorum's my delight,
It gars us a' in ane unite,
And ony fumph that keeps up fpite,
    In confcience I abhor him :
Blithe and merry we's be a'
        Blithe and merry,
        Blithe and merry,
Blithe and merry we's be a'
    To make a cheerfu' quorum ;
Blithe and merry we's be a'
As lang's we hae a breath to draw,
And dance, till we be like to fa',
    The reel of Tullochgorum.

There needs na be fo great a phrafe
Wi' dringing dull Italian lays ;

I wadna gi'e our ain Strathfpeys
For half a hundred fcore o'm.
They're dowf and dowie at the beft,
    Dowff and dowie,
    Dowff and dowie,
They're dowff and dowie at the beft,
    Wi' a' their variorum :
They're dowff and dowie at the beft,
Their allegro's, and a' the reft,
They canna pleafe a Highland tafte,
    Compar'd wi' Tullochgorum.

Let warldly minds themfelves opprefs
Wi' fear of want, and double cefs,
And filly fauls themfelves diftrefs
    Wi' keeping up decorum.
Shall we fae four and fulky fit,
    Sour and fulky,
    Sour and fulky,
Shall we fae four and fulky fit,
    Like auld Philofophorum ?
Shall we fae four and fulky fit,
Wi' neither fenfe, nor mirth, nor wit,
And canna rife to fhake a fit
    To the reel of Tullochgorum ?

May choiceft bleffings ftill attend
Each honeft-hearted open friend,
And calm and quiet be his end,
    Be a' that's good before him !

May peace and plenty be his lot,
 Peace and plenty,
 Peace and plenty,
May peace and plenty be his lot,
 And dainties a great ftore o'm :
May peace and plenty be his lot,
Unftain'd by any vicious blot !
And may he never want a groat
 That's fond of Tullochgorum.

But for the difcontented fool,
Who wants to be oppreffion's tool,
May envy gnaw his rotten foul,
 And blackeft fiends devour him !
May dole and forrow be his chance,
 Dole and forrow,
 Dole and forrow,
May dole and forrow be his chance,
 And honeft fouls abhor him :
My dole and forrow be his chance,
And a' the ills that come frae France,
Whoe'er he be that winna dance
 The reel of Tullochgorum.

G g

SONG CXXXVII.

SWEET POLL OF PLYMOUTH.

Sweet Poll of Plymouth was my dear, When

forc'd from her to go, ·Adown her cheeks rain'd

many a tear, My heart was fraught with woe

Our anchor weigh'd, for fea we ftood, The land

we left behind : Her tears then fwell'd the bri-

ney flood, My fighs encreas'd the wind. ·Our an-

chor weigh'd, for fea we ftood, The land we left

be-hind. Her tears then fwell'd the bri - - ny

flood, My fighs encreas'd the wind, My fighs

encreas'd the wind.

We plough'd the deep, and now between
   Us lay the ocean wide ;
For five long years I had not feen
   My fweet, my bonny bride ;
That time I fail'd the world around,
   All for my true-love's fake :
But, prefs'd, as we were homeward bound,
   I thought my heart would break.

The prefs-gang bold I afk'd in vain,
   To let me once on fhore ;
I long'd to fee my Poll again,
   But faw my Poll no more.

" And have they torn my love away ?
" And is he gone ?" she cried :
My Polly, sweetest flower of May,
She languish'd, droop'd, and died.

SONG CXXXVIII.

HENRY'S COTTAGE-MAID.

Ah where can fly my soul's true love ?

Sad   I   wan - der this lone grove ; Sighs

and tears for him   I   shed,   Hen - - ry

is   from Lau - - ra fled.   Thy love

to   me   thou didſt im-part, Thy love ſoon

won   my   vir - - - gin heart : But, deareſt

Henry, thou'ſt be - tray'd   Thy - - - love with

thy poor cottage maid.

Thro' the vale my grief appears,
Sighing ſad, with pearly tears :
Oft thy image is my theme,
As I wander on the green :
See, from my cheek the colour flies,
And love's ſweet hope within me dies ;
For oh ! dear Henry, thou'ſt betray'd
Thy love, with thy dear village-maid.

SONG CXXXIX.

ERE AROUND THE HUGE OAK.

Ere around the huge oak that o'erſhadows

yon mill, The fond i-vy had dar'd to entwine ;

Ere the church was a ru - in that nods on

the hill, Or a rook built his neſt on the pine,.

Or the rook built his neſt on the pine.

Could I trace back the time a far diftant date,
　Since my forefathers toil'd in this field ;
And the farm I now hold on your honour's eftate
　Is the fame that my grandfather till'd.
He, dying, bequeath'd to his fon a good name,
　Which unfullied defcended to me ;
For my child I've preferv'd it, unblemifh'd with
　　fhame,
　And it ftill from a fpot fhall be free.

SONG CXL.

JOHN OF BADENYON.

When firſt I came to be a man Of twenty years

or ſo, I thought myſelf a handſome youth, And

fain the world would know : In beſt attire I ſtept

abroad, With ſpirits briſk and gay, And here and

there and every where Was like a morn in May :

No care I had, nor fear of want, But rambled

up and down, And for a beau I might have pafs'd

in country or in town : I ftill was pleas'd where-

e'er I went, And when I was alone, I tun'd my

pipe, and pleas'd myfeil Wi' John of Badenyon.

Now in the days of youthful prime
   A miftrefs I muft find ;
For love, they fay, gives one an air,
   And even improves the mind :
On Phillis fair, above the reft,
   Kind fortune fix'd my eyes,
Her piercing beauty ftruck my heart,
   And fhe became my choice :
To Cupid, then, with hearty pray'r,
   I offer'd many a vow,
And danc'd, and fung, and figh'd, and fwore,
   As other lovers do :

But when at laſt I breath'd my flame,
I found her cold as ſtone ;
I left my girl, and tun'd my pipe
To John of Badenyon.

When love had thus my heart beguil'd
With fooliſh hopes and vain,
To friendſhip's port I ſteer'd my courſe,
And laugh'd at lover's pain.
A friend I got by lucky chance,
- 'Twas ſomething like divine ;
An honeſt friend's a precious gift,
And ſuch a gift was mine :
And now whatever might betide,
A happy man was I,
In any ſtrait I knew to whom
I freely might apply :
A ſtrait ſoon came, my friend I try'd,
He laugh'd and ſpurn'd my moan:
I hied me home, and pleas'd myſelf
With John of Badenyon.

I thought I ſhould be wiſer next,
And would a patriot turn ;
Began to doat on Johnny Wilkes,
And cry up Parſon Horne :
Their noble ſpirit I admir'd,
And prais'd their manly zeal,
Who had with flaming tongue and pen
Maintain'd the public weal :

But ere a month or two was paſt,
   I found myſelf betray'd;
'Twas ſelf and party after all,
   For all the ſtir they made.
At laſt I ſaw theſe factious knaves
   Inſult the very throne;
I curs'd them all, and tun'd my pipe
   To John of Badenyon.

What next to do, I mus'd a while,
   Still hoping to ſucceed;
I pitch'd on books for company,
   And gravely try'd to read;
I bought and borrow'd ev'ry where,
   And ſtudy'd night and day;
Nor miſt what dean or doctor wrote,
   That happen'd in my way:
Philoſophy I now eſteem'd
   The ornament of youth,
And carefully, thro' many a page,
   I hunted after truth:
A thouſand various ſchemes I tried,
   And yet was pleas'd with none:
I threw them by, and tun'd my pipe
   To John of Badenyon.

And now, ye youngſters, every where,
   Who want to make a ſhew,
Take heed in time, nor vainly hope
   For happineſs below:

What you may fancy pleafure here,
  Is but an empty name ;
For girls, and friends, and books are fo,
  You'll find them all the fame.
Then be advis'd, and warning take
  From fuch a man as me ;
I'm neither Pope, nor Cardinal,
  Nor one of low degree ;
You'll find difpleafure every where,
  Then do as I have done,
E'en tune your pipe, and pleafe yourfell
  Wi' John of Badenyon.

SONG CXLIII.

FAIR ROSALIE.

On that lone bank where Lubin died, Fair

Ro - fa - le, a wretched maid, Sat weeping o'er

the cruel tide, Faithful to her Luban's fhade :

" O may fome kind, fome gentle wave, Waft

him to this mournful fhore, Thefe tender hands

fhould make his grave, And deck his corps

H h

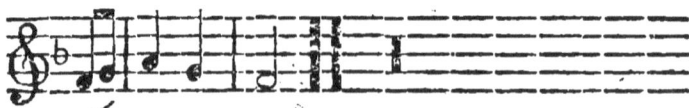

with flowers o'er.

" I'd ever watch his mould'ring clay,
  " And pray for his eternal reft ;
" When time his form has worn away,
  " His duft I'd place within my breaft !"
While thus fhe mourn'd her Lubin loft,
  And echo to her grief replied,
Lo ! at her feet his corps was toft !
  She fhriek'd !---fhe clafp'd him !--figh'd---and
  died !

SONG CXLIV.

THE LASS OF HUMBER-SIDE.

In lonely cot, by Humber-fide, I fit and

mourn my hours away ; For conftant Will was

Peggy's pride, And now he sleeps in Iceland

bay. Still as the ships pass to and fro, I fond-

ly lift to yo, ya, yo; Still as the ships pass to

and fro, I fondly lift to yo, ya, yo, Yo, ya,

yo, Yo, ya, yo, Yo, ya, yo, yo.

Six months on Greenland's icy coast,
　Where half the year is dreary night,
He toil'd for me, and oft would boast
　That Peggy was his sole delight.
　　Still as the ships, &c.

Ah! woe is me! I often cry,
  As thro' the broken panes I peep;
And as the diftant fails I fpy,
  I think of deareft Will and weep.
    Still as the fhips, &c.

If loud and fwelling ftorms I heard,
  As on my lonefome bed I lay'd,
All night alone for Will I fear'd
  All night for Will alone I pray'd.
    Still as the fhips, &c.

The bride-knot which my love did wear,
  Loofe hung a pendant o'er my door,
And when it told the wind was fair,
  I fancy'd foon he'd be on fhore.
    Still as the fhips, &c.

At length the very fhip I fpy'd,
  In which my conftant Will had fail'd,
With hafte I ran to Humber-fide,
  And loud and oft the failors hail'd:
    The deck they travers'd to and fro,
    And anfwer'd nought but yo, ya, yo.

The boatfwain, now, full near the fhore,
  I afk for Will,---he fhook his head:
I fear, faid I, he is no more---
  His anfwer was, " Poor Will is dead !"
    Ah me ! I fell, opprefs'd with woe !
    And heard no more their yo, ya, yo.

SONG CXLVI.

THE UNION OF BACCHUS AND VENUS.

I'm a vot'ry of Bacchus, his Godſhip adore,

And love at his ſhrine gay libations to pour,

And Venus, bleſt Venus, my boſom inſpires, For

ſhe lights in our ſouls the moſt ſacred of fires. Yet

to neither I ſwear ſole allegiance to hold, My

bottle and laſs I by turns muſt enfold: For

H h 3

the ſweeteſt of unions that mortals can prove,

Is of Bacchus, gay god, and the goddeſs of love :

For the ſweeteſt of unions that mortals can

prove, Is of Bacchus, gay god, and the goddeſs

of love.

When fill'd to the fair the briſk bumper I hold,
Can the miſer ſurvey with ſuch pleaſure his gold ?
The ambroſia of gods no ſuch reliſh can boaſt,
If good Port fill your glaſs, and fair Kitty's the toaſt :
And the charms of your girl more angelic will be,
If her ſopha's encircl'd with wreaths from his tree.

For the fweeteft of unions that mortals can prove,
Is of Bacchus, gay god, and the goddefs of love.

All partial diftin&ions I hate from my foul :
O give me my fair one, and give me my bowl!
Blifs reflefted from either will fend to my heart
Ten thoufand fweet joys which they can't have apart.
Go, try it, ye fmiling and gay looking throng,
And your hearts fhall in unifon beat to my fong,
That the fweeteft of unions that mortals can prove,
Is of Bacchus, gay god, and the goddefs of love.

SONG CXLVII.

SUNG AT

THE ANNUAL GENERAL MEETING

OF

ST ANDREW'S SOCIETY, ABERDEEN,

November 30th, 1790.

All hail to the day that auſpicious returns,

Our country's bleak regions to cheer ! Tho' Na-

ture the winter's wild ravages mourns, Let joy ſhed

its influence here : Far hence be the frowns and

the murmurs of care, Let each breaſt catch the pa-

triot flame. What ſoul but aſpires in our raptures

to ſhare, When Scotia and Freedom's the

theme, When Scotia and Freedom's the

theme.

Tho' cold are our hills, and tho' barren our plains,
   Our climate tho' rude and ſevere,
Yet health, roſy health, ſtrings the nerves of our
     ſwains,
   And ſmiles on the cheeks of our fair;
And Freedom, bleſt Freedom, the gift of a god,
   From regions more fertile exil'd,
'Mid our woods and our wilds had of old her abode,
   And our clime of its rigours beguil'd.

In hoſtile array when Rome's legions appear'd,
   Her voice ſounded loud o'er the heath;
On our hills her proud ſtandard exulting ſhe rear'd,
   And her motto was " Conqueſt or death."
Our anceſtors heard, and re-choed the ſounds,
   " To conquer or die be our doom !"

Unmov'd as their mountains, 'twas theirs to fet
    bounds,
To the pow'r and ambition of Rome·

Their laurels, bequeath'd from the fire to the fon,
    Thro' ages unfading have bloom'd ;
The rays of their glory unclouded have fhone.
And their country's bleak fhores have illum'd.
What heroes unnumber'd have clouded the fcene,
    Well Europe's proud annals can tell !
For Freedom, regardlefs of danger and pain,
    How they fought, how they bled, how they fell !

And now that the tempeft of war o'er the land,
    No more fpreads its kindling alarms,
In the foft cares of peace let us join hand in hand,
    And in arts be as great as in arms.
Supported by Freedom, may Commerce encreafe,
    And our fhores her rich treafures invite,
May Science, extending the bleffings of Peace,
    Diffufe the mild beams of her light.

And lo ! where a wreath of unfading renown
    For St Andrew the Virtues entwine,--
Thofe virtues, protected by him that have grown,
    Round his head fhedding luftre divine :
O'er the pale cheek of poverty long be it ours
    Again to fhed health's rofy bloom ;
And the eye that the torrent of mifery pours,
    With joy and with hope to relume.

'Mong nations the firft, as in Freedom in worth,
  May Caledon ftill be proclaim'd :
Her daughters as bright as the morn of the North,
  And her fons as their forefathers fam'd :
Let the tools of a faction, the minions of pow'r,
  Court the fmiles of Ambition and Wealth ;
Her favours on flaves partial Fortune may fhow'r,
  Be ours Independence and Health.

Nor let the cold wifh by a Briton be breath'd,
  Which from felfifh affection has birth ;
Thofe bleffings to us by our fathers bequeath'd,
  May they cheer all the nations on earth !
May Fame's loudeft trump to each region proclaim,
  That the reign of the defpot fhall ceafe !
And mankind fhall welcome, with joyous acclaim,
  The æra of Freedom of Peace !

F I N I S.

Edinburgh :
PRINTED BY GRANT & MOIR,
PATERSON'S COURT.

Books printed for and fold by

SILVESTER DOIG, ROYAL EXCHANGE.

THE DUTY AND OFFICE

OF

A MESSENGER AT ARMS,

12mo, Price 5s. 6d. Bound.

- GRAMMATICAL EXERCISES,

18mo, Price 1s.

THE HISTORY OF SINGING BIRDS,

Adorned with 25 entire New Engravings,

12mo, Price 3s. neatly bound.

DECISIONS

OF THE COURT OF SESSION, FROM 1698 TO 1718,

Collected by Sir Hew Dalrymple,

Folio, Price 16s bound in Calf.

DECISIONS

OF THE COURT OF SESSION, FROM 1681 TO 1691,

Colllected by Sir Roger Hog of Harçarfe,

Folio, Price 18s. bound in Calf.

AND,

In the Prefs, and fpeedily will be publifhed,

A

NEW EDITION

OF

THE WORKS OF SHAKESPEARE,

In 8 Vols 12mo, 1 l. 4 s. bound in Calf.

www.ingramcontent.com/pod-product-compliance
Lightning Source LLC
Chambersburg PA
CBHW030908270326
41929CB00008B/611